Sit Down At His Table

Take Time To Enjoy His Presence

RSI
PUBLISHING

Dennis L Taylor

Scriptures are taken from the New International Version of the Bible
Books may be ordered through booksellers or by contacting:
Dennis Taylor
luke252.dennis@gmail.com

Raising the Standard International Publishing L. L. C.
https://www.rsipublishing.com
Navarre, Florida

ISBN: 9781960641205
Printed in the United States of America
Edition Date: August 2023

Contents

Dedication

I want to dedicate this devotional book to my two girls, Carsen Pablico and Mackenzie Poston. They are my heartbeat, and I could never tell them how much I love them. I watched them both being born and have tried my best to walk beside them in every situation. It is an honor to be called their dad. I thank God daily for the gift of such beautiful, talented, and gifted girls. I look back, and I wonder where the time went. They grow up too fast.

So many memories are flashing as I type out this dedication. It is like God is shoving pictures of the past right in front of my face. I remember those first days of each school year; they were always such a big deal: the new clothes, the new lunch box, and the excitement of having a new teacher. What about those Easter dresses with the crazy hairdo Mom created each year? There were times when I wanted to hug them forever, but there were also those times I could have pinched their head off. If you are a parent, you know what I am talking about.

I think about the endless soccer games and practices, sitting in a portable chair, watching their every move, and talking about what they need to work on or what they did well. I sometimes got out of hand during tight games. But I loved every minute, even the long trips, the countless money for club soccer, and the car's gas. I hope they know how proud I was when they signed their college scholarships and pursued their dreams. We overcame all the injuries, setbacks, letdowns, and difficult situations.

I must repeat it. Where did the time go? How did the time slip away so fast? From walking them across the parking lot to walking them down the aisle to handing you over to the man of your dreams. I love talking about our memories and reminiscing, but I am more excited about their future. God has His hand on my two girls; I know they will make a difference in this world. Sometimes life can be a struggle but hang on to the hand of Christ, and He will hold you tight in the storms of life. Never give up, back down, and surrender fully to Christ.

Girls, know how much I love you. No day goes by when I don't pray for you both. I pray that you both will grow in your walk with the Lord. I pray that He will bless your marriage and my future grandbabies!

I look forward to what God has in store for you both.

Dream big, pray bigger!

Dad

~ 1 ~

Fitting In Or Sticking Out?

I want to share a quick word with you today and leave you with a question to answer. My heart and passion are encouraging others in their walk with Christ. God has called me to spend the last third of my life spreading hope and encouragement and pushing people closer to Him. But I also want Christians to stop and think about how they are investing their lives. Seeing so many friends walking away from the Church and living a life that doesn't glorify the Lord breaks my heart. So many other things have become more important to them than their relationship with Christ. It is so easy to get lost in our selfishness and to run after all the wrong things. I have been there and done that, and I know how easy it is to fall into that trap.

I am not calling people out or trying to condemn you; I want to encourage you to look at where you are spiritually and ask yourself, how did I get back here? How did you return to what you pursued before turning your life over to Jesus? Somehow you have left the side of the One who died for you, followed the things of this world, and lost sight of Jesus. I want to share the words of Jesus that are found in Luke 4:18-19 when Jesus said:

> *"The Spirit of the Lord is on me because he has anointed me to preach the good news to the poor. He has sent me to proclaim freedom for prisoners and recovery of sight for the blind, to release the oppressed, to proclaim the year of the Lord's favor."*

This passage reveals what drove Jesus and reveals His passion for life. In other words, this was the heart and soul of why He came to die. Is this your passion for life? Is this what drives you as a believer? Are lives being changed around you? Are you just fitting in, or is your life sticking out? Dare to be different and pursue the heart of Christ. Jesus gave us an example to follow and showed us how to live a life that pleases God. How are you doing so far?

~2~

Stop Signs

Have you ever rolled through a stop sign? You may think, that's no big deal; I always do that. However, not only have I rolled through a stop sign, but I have also driven right past one and never slowed down, and I didn't realize it until I went through that intersection. Thank God no one was coming from the other direction; that could have been a bad situation.

In this life, we are running wide open, making decisions without thinking everything through or even pausing to pray over each situation. Think about it this way; stop signs are placed in specific spots for a reason. This life can get crazy, and the demands will push you to your limits. There will be times when God will place a stop sign in front of you and put it there for our protection. In Exodus 18, Moses knew something had to change, or he would fall apart trying to manage all the demands of his life. Moses became responsible for hearing the Israelites' problems and handing down judgments. He did this every day, all day long.

Moses' father-in-law gave him some great advice in Exodus 18:17-19 and said:

> *"What you are doing is not good. You and these people who come to you will only wear yourselves out. The work is too heavy for you; you cannot handle it alone. Listen to me and I will give you some advice, and may God be with you. You must be the people's*

representative before God and bring their disputes to him."

Can you relate to that? Are you juggling knives, and it feels impossible to keep going? Instead of Moses taking all that responsibility upon himself, he shared his duties and stopped trying to do everything himself. So many times, we must let go of what we've been holding to receive what God wants to give us. Watch those stop signs; they are there for a reason.

-3-

Balanced Life

Life can be challenging, and hard times will hit us from every side. I loved playing High School football, but sometimes our game plan didn't work well. There were times of confusion and frustration, and I didn't know what to do next. So, I called a timeout. That would stop the clock, and the game would be paused. That gave me time to talk with the coach, rethink our situation, and take a deep breath. But in real life, there are no timeouts. Life doesn't stop when things get hard or don't go as planned.

Do you have lost dreams, or maybe you have experienced disappointments and heartaches? Have you ever wondered, what if? There are many times when I wish I could go back in time and change a few things. Correct some poor decisions, or put more effort into what I did then. We all have regrets. But we can't live life looking backward. We must keep moving forward positively, facing obstacles and climbing over them. Hitting hard times but not turning back or quitting. That is one thing I struggled with early in life. I would give up or leave if things didn't go my way. When something wasn't easy, or I was facing adversity, instead of stepping up or meeting the challenge. I found it a lot easier to quit. I also struggled with balance and inconsistency in my life. I could do one thing well while other areas of my life fell apart. I am not alone; many of you struggle with this issue today.

Luke 2:52 has changed my life forever and I want to share it with the world. This verse says, "Jesus grew in wisdom and stature, and in favor with God and men."

Jesus grew in every area of life. He had a balanced life. Jesus is the TOTAL PACKAGE. He is our ultimate example of how to live life. I encourage you to examine your life and ask these simple questions: Am I growing in wisdom? Am I taking good care of my physical body? Am I growing in my relationship with my Heavenly Father? Do I have healthy relationships with my family and those I work with? God calls you to be that total package who possesses a balanced life.

-4-

Fill Up

Christmas is one of my favorite times of the year. December tends to fly by, and everything seems like a blur. But it is so sweet to slow down every morning, take in God's goodness, and refocus on what is most important, my relationship with my Heavenly Father. I encourage you today to take your cares and worries to the Lord in prayer and leave them at His feet. Dive into the Word of God and get lost in His amazing grace. Worship Him, and soak in His presence, but don't be in a hurry to rush away.

> *Psalm 84:10-12: "Better is one day in your courts than a thousand elsewhere; I would rather be a doorkeeper in the house of my God than dwell in the tents of the wicked. For the Lord God is a sun and shield; the Lord bestows favor and honor; no good thing does he withhold from those whose walk is blameless. O God Almighty, blessed is the man who trusts in you."*

Recharge your spiritual batteries today, pull into God's soul-filling station, and ask Him to fill you up! Know this; He will only fill you with the best stuff. So, yes, take time during this Christmas season to fuel up with the things of God, but make sure you give it away too. Let others see Jesus in you. Don't allow the business to rob you of joy and peace. Don't waste your time on the cheap gas the world offers you, but only fill up with the good stuff that comes only through a personal relationship with Jesus Christ. God bless you today.

~5~
Joy To The World

Joy to the world, the Lord has come! He didn't come as a conquering king but as a baby and was named Jesus. He should have been worshiped and adored, but man despised and rejected him.

> Isaiah 53:4-7 tells us, "Surely he took our infirmities and carried our sorrows, yet we considered him stricken by God, smitten by him, and afflicted. But he was pierced for our transgressions, he was crushed for our iniquities; the punishment that brought us peace was upon him, and by his wounds, we are healed. We all, like sheep, have gone astray, each of us has turned to his own way, and the Lord has laid on him the iniquities of us all. He was oppressed and afflicted, yet he did not open his mouth; he was led like a lamb to the slaughter."

Again I say joy to the world, the Lord has come, and his name is Jesus! Jesus was the only man born to die. Because of Jesus's birth, death, and resurrection, we can all experience peace, joy, and eternal life with the Father.

> John 3:16-17: "For God so loved the world that he gave his one and only Son, that whoever believes in him shall not perish but have everlasting life. For God did not send his Son into the world to condemn the world, but to save the world through him."

I encourage you to celebrate Jesus and what he did for us many years ago. He overcame sin and death; in other words, he took our place on the cross. We deserve those nails, we deserve that beating, and we deserve that crown of thorns. But he didn't open his mouth and took our place on an old rugged cross. The baby in the manger, the world's Savior, the King of kings, and the Lord of lords, took our place on the cross. Joy to the world, the Lord has come! Take time today, and thank your Heavenly Father for the baby Jesus, and give Him some praise.

~6~

Celebrate His Goodness

The message of Jesus is in full bloom, and I can't wait to see what God will do. I want to encourage believers to look around daily, keep their spiritual eyes open, and be prepared to share their faith with acts of kindness and grace. Please don't get caught up in words of negativity that the world wants to spill into our schools, neighborhoods, and our cities. God is moving and working behind the scenes to reach those who have never received His grace.

> *Romans 12:21 says, "Do not be overcome by evil, but overcome evil with good."*

Listen, greater is He that is in you than He that is in the world. Because of Christ in us, we are overcomers, and we are on the winning team. So Christmas is our time to celebrate and enjoy the goodness of the Lord. But it is also the season to go and tell and let the world know about our King. So here is a message for the Church today from the pen of Paul.

> *Romans 13:11-14: "The hour has come for you to wake up from your slumber, because salvation is nearer now than when we first believed. The night is nearly over; the day is almost here. So let us put aside the deeds of darkness and put on the armor of light. Let us behave decently, as in the daytime, not in orgies and drunkenness, not in sexual immorality and*

debauchery, not in dissension and jealousy. Rather, clothe yourselves with the Lord Jesus Christ, and so not think how to gratify the desires of the sinful nature."

Hope is here; Jesus left the splendor of heaven to be born in a lowly manger. He overcame sin and death and sat at the Lord's right hand. He is the Savior of the world and worthy of being praised. So wake up Church from your slumber, clothe yourselves with Jesus, and tell everybody you know about His amazing love.

~7~
Need Rest?

That are you resting in? Where do you find comfort? What or whom do you lean on when everything seems to fall apart? Where do you go to find rest when your favorite football team loses, or your money runs out before all your bills are paid?

> David wrote Psalm 62:1-2, saying, "My soul finds rest in God alone; my salvation comes from him. He alone is my rock and my salvation; he is my fortress, I will never be shaken."

We live in a world that never seems to sleep. There is always an activity to attend or a party to go to. What happened to the forty-hour work week? What happened to just having one job? Our bills are taking over, and the pressure of life is growing to the point of ballooning where it is about to pop. Then there are always family issues. For some reason, they never seem to go away; there must always be some drama. With everything piling up, where do you go for rest? Have you ever wanted to return to bed and pull the covers over your head?

When trouble time comes, and life seems overwhelming, don't turn to a bowl of ice cream or a bottle of wine; turn to your Heavenly Father and rest in His presence. In His arms, you will find comfort; in His arms, you will find peace; and in His arms, you will find refuge.

Jeremiah 33:11 says, "Give thanks to the Lord Almighty, for the Lord is good; his love endures forever."

I challenge you to say this verse ten times out loud in a prayer of thanksgiving to the Father. Thank Him for His provision, thank Him for His mercy, and thank Him for loving you. Where do you run to find rest? Run to the very One who gives life.

~8~

Overcome Worry

What are you filling your mind with today? What do you constantly think about, and where is your stress level? The holidays are usually the craziest time of the year because we pack our schedules so full that we can never say no. Don't you wish we could turn our minds on and off like a light switch? Have you ever stayed awake at night and can't stop thinking about a particular family issue, unpaid bills, a broken relationship, or worried about what someone thought about you? At some time or another, we have all been there. I want to share some scripture that has helped me not to over-worry and stress and to know the secret of the peace of God.

> Philippians 4:4-7 says this, "Rejoice in the Lord always. I say it again: Rejoice! Let your gentleness be evident to all. The Lord is near. Do not be anxious about anything, but in everything, by prayer and petition, with thanksgiving, present your request to God. And the peace of God, will transcend all understanding, and will guard your hearts and minds in Christ Jesus."

I challenge you today to turn your phone off entirely and put it in another room if you have to. Turn up the worship music and get lost in the presence of God. Set aside 30 minutes to an hour, just you and the Lord. Then rejoice in His goodness, telling Him, "Thank you" for every blessing of life, give Him all your cares and worries, and trust Him with them. Then pray for the peace of God to fall on you like the morning dew. Guard your hearts and minds against the enemy. Don't back down or stop fighting. Take your eyes off that situation and turn them to the King of kings. Stop dwelling on the negative and focus on the love of Christ. Rejoice, rejoice, and again I say rejoice!

> Philippians 4:8-9, "Finally, brothers, whatever is true, whatever is noble, whatever is right, whatever is pure, whatever is lovely, whatever is admirable-if anything is excellent or praiseworthy-think about such things. Whatever you have learned or received or heard from me, or seen in me, put it into practice. And the God of peace will be with you."

~9~

Are You Listening?

Are you listening to the instructions the Lord shares with you daily? Is your heart in tune with the Heavenly Father, or are you doing your own thing? Do you ever feel like you are fighting an uphill battle but are bound and determined to make it work, no matter what? Jeremiah listened closely to the Father's voice, paid close attention, and followed God's instructions.

> *Jeremiah 18:1-2, "This is the word that came to Jeremiah from the Lord: Go down to the potter's house, and there I will give you my message."*

Jeremiah was prepared to hear God's voice; he had a listening ear and a pure heart. So what did Jeremiah do when he heard the voice of God? He did exactly what God told him to do; he was obedient.

> *Jeremiah 18:3-6, "So I went down to the potter's house, and I saw him working at the wheel. But the pot was marred in his hands; so the potter formed it into another pot, shaping it as it seemed best for him. Then the word of the Lord came to me: 'O house of Israel, can I not do with you as this potter does?' declares the Lord. 'Like clay in the hand of the potter, so are you in my hand.'"*

Here is the question I want you to think about; Did the clay have the right to tell the potter what to make it? Of course not, but how often do we ignore what God is trying to shape us into or form us to be? Look what the Lord said in Jeremiah 18:11-12:

> *"So turn from your evil ways, each one of you, and reform your ways and actions. But they will reply, "It's of no use. We will continue with our own plans; each of us will follow the stubbornness of his evil heart."*

Man, we can be stubborn and hard-headed; it has to drive God crazy. We think we know what is best for us, ignore God's instructions, and do it our way, no matter what. Surrender your heart and will to the Father today. Stop beating your head against the wall and trying to force something to work and give God complete control. Let Him have His way with you, and begin to enjoy the goodness of God. His plans are best because He holds the future.

~10~

The Preserved Life

Mrs. Jean Ragan is one of the sweetest people you will ever meet, and she can make some of the best blackberry jellies you will ever put in your mouth. Put that jelly on a toast; it will make you smile all day. It is that good. It's incredible to me how someone can take a Blackberry that is about to fall to the ground and rot away and preserve it, and some six months later, it's still sitting in my refrigerator and bringing me so much joy! She has found a way to preserve a blackberry, maintain it, or keep it alive. Those blackberries are prepared for long-term storage.

> *Psalm 119:40 says this, "How I long for your precepts! Preserve my life in your righteousness."*

In other words, God's precepts and righteousness preserve us; He keeps us alive and prepares us for long-term storage if you know what I mean. So, I want to continue encouraging you to pray the scripture daily! Don't push it away or come up with some weak excuses.

> *Psalm 119:33-37, "Teach me, O Lord, to follow your decrees; then I will keep them to the end. Give me understanding, and I will keep your law and obey it with all my heart. Direct me in the path of your commands, for there I find delight. Turn my heart towards your statutes and not towards my selfish*

19

gain. Turn my eyes away from worthless things; preserve my life according to your word."

"Lord, thanks for preserving me through the blood of Jesus Christ." I encourage you to take an extra five minutes to praise the Lord for the gift of salvation and His goodness shown to you through His Son.

~11~

Kindness Of God

Have you ever slowed down long enough to think about the kindness of God? How can we wrap our minds around that and fully appreciate what the Lord has done for us? Where do we even begin to say thank you? My parents made so many sacrifices when I was growing up. We didn't have much money, but we didn't know it. Instead, we had everything we needed: love, support, and God-centered home life. I could tell you story after story of how my parents showed kindness to my sister, brother, and myself, but this devotion couldn't contain it.

I remember my mom cooking fried chicken, and boy was it good. Everyone in our family picked out their favorite piece of chicken, while mom always ended up with the back or a wing. She never complained and ate it with a smile. She did all the work, yet she gave her family the best part of the chicken. Did I take her kindness for granted? I sure did, but I don't know why. Pause this morning to think about the heart of God and take time to say thank you. My mom gave up a prime piece of chicken, but God gave up His Son.

Psalm 118:29: "Give thanks to the Lord, for he is good; his love endures forever."

Celebrate God's kindness today and let the people around you know how good He is. Thank you, Lord, for your loving kindness. What He has blessed you with, turn around and give it away.

Colossians 3:12-13 tells us this, "Put on then, as God's chosen ones, holy and beloved, compassionate hearts, kindness, humility, meekness, and patience, bearing one another, if one has a complaint against another, forgiving each other, as the Lord has forgiven you, so you also must forgive."

God is so good.

~12~

Waiting

Have you ever felt like God wasn't there, or maybe He has forgotten about you? I think we all have at some time or another. Believe me, when I say this, God is always working behind the scenes, and it is always for our good. But God never gets in a hurry, but we do. We don't like waiting, do we? Fast food is never fast enough, the microwave takes too long, and Christmas seems like it will never get here. I get so tired of waiting! But Christmas isn't about the rush and the business of the season; Christmas is about a promise fulfilled. God has come through for us, and He is faithful. This is what Advent is all about; it's about the arrival of a notable person or an event. It's about expectantly waiting, hopefully anticipating, and joyful preparation. So you see, Christmas is a season of hope.

> *Luke 2:11 says, "Today in the town of David a Savior has been born to you, he is Christ the Lord." Israel had been waiting on a coming King. They had hopeful anticipation that He could deliver them from bondage and set them free. They were asking, "When will our King get here?"*

On the right day, in the right place, and at the right time, Jesus arrived! If you are waiting today, take hope in the manger and know that God loves and adores you. Galatians 4:4-5 tells us this:

"But when the time had fully come, God sent his Son, born of a woman, born under law, to redeem those under the law, that we might receive the full right of sons."

An old saying goes like this: "Good things come to those who wait." Unfortunately, I am not very patient, and that statement used to get on my nerves badly. But there is much truth in that statement.

Isaiah 30:18 says, "Yet the Lord longs to be gracious to you; he rises to show you compassion. For the Lord is a God of justice. Blessed are all who wait for him."

Knowing this truth reveals that good things come to those who wait on the Lord.

~13~

Not Resting?

I have so many things to do. I have meetings to go to, a mile-long checklist, and so many emails to send out. Last night, I went to bed thinking about everything I had to do today, which is unusual for me. Most nights, when my head hits the pillow, I am out till the alarm goes off. I tossed and turned for hours, and I finally fell asleep. This morning, I was tempted to bypass my time alone with God to get an early start on my to-do list. But God pushed me to His Word and nourished me for my day. It's amazing how God's goodness can change your focus and outlook in minutes.

> *I turned to Psalm 119:133-136 which says, "Direct my footsteps according to your word; let no sin rule over me. Redeem me from the oppression of men, that I may obey your precepts. Make your face shine upon your servant and teach me your decree."*

You may have a day like mine and already go 90 miles an hour. I encourage you to stop for a few minutes and pray this scripture to your Heavenly Father. Ask Him to direct your footsteps today and to redeem you. Also, pray that you can walk in obedience in the craziness of your busy life and ask Him to smile on you today. Praying scripture will change your perspective and your mindset today.

I challenge you to read and memorize Matthew 11:28-29 which says:

"Come to me, all who are weary and burdened, and I will give you rest. Take my yoke upon you and learn of me, for I am gentle and humble in heart, and you will find rest for your souls."

Need rest? Did life overcome him? Come to Jesus, lean on Him, trust Him, and He will carry your load. He will save you a lot of heartache and burdens.

~14~

The True Light

Thanksgiving was awesome. I am so grateful for a few days off and time spent with family and friends in Georgia. It is always good to take time to reflect and tell God "thank you" for the blessings of life. As Thanksgiving time is closing out, the doors of Christmas swing wide open. It's the most beautiful time of the year, more time off, presents, great food, and time again with family. But we know that's not what makes Christmas special.

> *John 1:9-14 says, "The true light that gives light to every man was coming into the world. He was in the world, and through him, the world did not recognize him. He came to that which was his own, but his own did not receive him. Yet to all who receive him, to those who believe in his name, he gave the right to become children of God, children born not of natural descent, nor of human decision or a husband's will, but born of God. The Word became flesh and made a dwelling among us. We have seen his glory, the glory of the One and Only, who came from the Father, full of grace and truth."*

Jesus came to earth to give his life for us, to die on a rugged cross, and to be buried in a borrowed tomb. But thank God he didn't stay in that tomb but arose from the grave! He overcame sin and death and now sits at the Father's right hand. We have LIFE today because of what Jesus did so long ago. The Creator of the world placed His

LIGHT IN ME! Now it is time to light this world up and to let your LIGHT SHINE. Tell someone today about the difference Jesus has made in your life, and celebrate His goodness.

~15~
Shake It Off

I love it when life is going smoothly, and everything seems to fall right into place. I don't know about you, but that is a rarity. How many times have we faced difficulties, conflict, and disappointment? If you let it, life can leave you beat up, discouraged, and overwhelmed. Sometimes in the struggle, we tend to become tired and want to roll over and throw our hands up. You may take good shots from this old world but don't lose hope. Keep fighting.

I want to encourage you today to shake it off and take your eyes off the negative stuff that is going on around you. Right now, thank God for three things you are blessed with. Then stand up, don't coward down, and feel helpless during a battle. Whether you know it or not, you are in a spiritual warfare. Stand up and fight. Then look up, and realize where your true strength comes from.

> Second Corinthians 4:8-9 says, "We are hard pressed on every side, but not crushed, perplexed, but not in despair; persecuted, but not abandoned; struck down, but not destroyed."

We are overcomers in Christ Jesus. Therefore do not lose heart or back down. Instead, shake it off, stand up, look up, and let the Lord fight for you.

> Romans 8:31-32 tells us, "What, then, shall we say in response to this? If God is for us, who can be against

us? He who did not spare his own Son, but gave him up for us all how will he not also, along with him, graciously give us all things?"

We will have trials and challenging times, but remember that God loves us and has our back. So knock the dust off and keep moving forward. God bless you today.

~16~

His Invitation

I received Christ into my life when I was five years old. Did I fully understand what all that truly meant? No, but I knew I needed a Savior. The older I get, the more I pray for wisdom. God opens the window of truth wider and wider about the invitation I received nearly fifty years ago. The God of the universe has offered an invitation to all who will call Him Lord to meet with us daily and share our needs and concerns. Listen, God is on call 24 hours a day, seven days a week, fifty-two weeks a year. He is there for you and cares about your life's most intimate details. Not only does He care about your concerns and needs, but He also wants us to know Him.

> *Philippians 2:1-2 says this, "If you have any encouragement from being united in Christ, if any comfort from his love, if any fellowship with the Spirit, if any tenderness and compassion, then make my joy complete by being like-minded, having the same love, being one in spirit and purpose."*

What an invitation, but God's invitation doesn't stop here. That invitation I received fifty years ago is also an invitation to participate with Him in His eternal purpose. How unbelievable is that?

> *Ephesians 3:10-11 tells us, "His intent was that now, through the Church, the manifold wisdom of God*

should be made known to the rulers and authorities in the heavenly realm, according to His eternal purpose which he accomplished in Christ Jesus our Lord."

Are you overwhelmed yet by His invitation to little ole you? But He doesn't stop there; by opening the door to Christ, He also invites us to partner with Him in all His ways. Think about that, we are called into a partnership with the One who owns it all! Life's ultimate privilege is that we can know God intimately through fellowship. God is calling us on an adventure, and He has thrown open the window of opportunity to experience more of Him and His goodness. It's time for us to get out of the kiddie pool, take the arm floaters off, and jump into the deep waters of fellowship with the King of the universe. Discovering and embracing His ways will require a lifetime.

~17~
Get Ready To Run

All believers in Christ have been rescued and placed at our race's starting point. Our rescue was incredible; we had been forgiven and freed from our past sins and mess-ups. But being a Christian involves more than a "rescue operation." There is a race to run, a life purpose to fulfill. For our new life in Christ to have real meaning, value, and direction, we must do more than look back at our rescue; we must look forward to life's purpose.

Second Timothy 1:8-9 says, "You are not rescued because of His grace, but you were rescued that you might fulfill His purpose."

Oh, how we must ask God to awaken our hearts to this truth today. Too often, Christians become "rescued-centered" and forget that we are called to run a life that will glorify the Heavenly Father. The critical question now is, when will we move past a preoccupation with our rescue and become occupied with running the race to fulfill God's eternal purpose?

Are you living out what God has called you to do? Are you still standing at the starting line with your hands on your hips? It's great to reflect and to be grateful for what Christ has done for us all, but it is time to run. It's time to fulfill your purpose! It's time to glorify God with your life. What you need is important, but what God receives is most important. So today, I dare you to drop to your knees and pray, "God, I want more." Don't be so preoccupied with your needs, wants, and problems. Keep your eyes on the prize of knowing Christ and Him glorified. Let's run in such a way that it will make our Heavenly Father smile. Get ready to run Church.

~18~

Fellowship With Who?

What is fellowship? Fellowship is a friendly association, especially with people who share one's interests. A group of people meeting to pursue a shared interest or aim. That is the textbook definition, but my description sounds slightly different. Fellowship is a gathering of friends who come together for a meal to enjoy each other's company. It's a time to share life's struggles and heartache and enjoy laughs, and it's a time of doing life together.

The God of the universe invites all His children to a private appointment to enter His presence for unrestricted fellowship. What a privilege! Life's ultimate freedom is wrapped up in this word: FELLOWSHIP. The Creator of heaven and earth desires to meet with me daily, and His door is open to me twenty-four hours a day. To see a doctor, you must make an appointment and possibly wait a few weeks to get in.

First John 1:3: "Our fellowship is with the Father, and with His Son Jesus Christ."

We can commune with Him immediately, not waiting in line. Again, what a privilege we have as a child of the living God. As if that wasn't enough, because we are blessed with His fellowship, we can also participate in His purpose and become ministry partners with the very Creator of heaven and earth. If that doesn't get you jacked, something is wrong with your order of passions.

Philippians 3:10: "I want to know Christ and the power of His resurrection and the fellowship of sharing in His suffering."

I want to encourage you to enjoy some good ole fashion fellowship with the One who loves you the most. Don't be in a rush, and make sure you listen more than you talk.

~19~

Judge Not

Christians are accountable to each other, whether we like it or not. We all need that accountability. But we are also quick to judge others which God has not called us to do.

> *James 5:16: "Confess your sins to each other and pray for each other so that you may be healed. The prayer of a righteous man is powerful and effective."*

> *Paul wrote in First Corinthians 5:12-13 and said, "What business is it of mine to judge those outside the church? Are you not to judge those inside? God will judge those outside."*

Few things discredit the church more in the mind of unbelievers than when he holds them accountable to a standard they never acknowledged. How crazy is that? Think about it, Christians expect non-Christians to behave like Christians when half the Christians don't act like it half the time.

> *Colossians 4:5-6 says, "Be wise in the way you act towards outsiders, make the most of every opportunity. Let your conversation be always full of grace, seasoned with salt, so that you may know how to answer everyone."*

Put on the eyes of Jesus and look beyond what your human eyes can see. Look past the bad behavior, the filthy mouth, and the rudeness. Behind every attitude is a story. Possibly a story of hurt, defeat, and rejection.

> *Matthew 9:35-36 says, "Jesus went through all the towns and villages, teaching in their synagogues, preaching the good news of the kingdom and healing every disease and sickness. When he saw the crowds, he had compassion on them, because they were harassed and helpless, like a sheep without a shepherd."*

See through the eyes of Christ, don't pass judgment or condemn others. Thank the Lord for three unbelieving friends today. Then ask the Lord for an opportunity to share your story with them.

~20~

Exposed To The Glory

Take time today to tell God "thank you" for the blessings of life. I also encourage you to look at God's goodness and grace and take your eyes off yourself long enough to see His glory.

> *Lamentation 3:22-26 Jeremiah says, "Because of the Lord's great love we are not consumed, for his compassions never fail. They are new every morning; great is your faithfulness. I say to myself, 'The Lord is my portion; therefore I will wait for him.' The Lord is good to those whose hope is in him, it is good to wait quietly for the salvation of the Lord."*

Seeing His glory and goodness will cause us to examine our lives and push us to a time of confession. The light exposes things in the dark.

> *Jeremiah writes in Lamentation 3:40-42 and says, "Let us examine our ways and test them, and let us return to the Lord. Let us lift up our hearts and our hands to God in heaven, and say; "We have sinned and rebelled, and you have not forgiven."*

Look at His goodness, confess your heart's sin, and receive His grace today.

First John 1:9 says, "If we confess our sins, he is faithful and just and will forgive us our sins and purify us from all unrighteousness."

That is good news and a promise from Jesus Himself that we can hold on to in our time of weakness and sin. We all have fallen short and sinned at some time or another. But thanks be to God; His grace is sufficient for me, and mercy is new every day.

Make time to spend with the Light of the world, soak in His presence and seek His face. Let Him have free reign in your life, and allow Him to light the darkest corner of your heart. Then experience the joy He will bring to your life.

~21~
Just A Question

Paul asked in Romans 8:35, "Who shall separate us from the love of Christ? Shall trouble or hardship or persecution or famine or nakedness or danger or sword?"

Think about it this morning: we all hit hard times and have failures and struggles. Fear and doubt love to come in and trip us up. Paul goes on and answers his question in the following few verses; listen to the truth he shares with us today in Romans 8:38-39:

"For I am convinced that neither death nor life, neither angels nor demons, neither the present or the future, nor any powers, neither height nor depth, nor anything else in all of creation, will be able to separate us from the love of God that is in Christ Jesus our Lord."

If that isn't good news, I don't know what is. The Creator of the universe loves us! Can you grasp that? Try to wrap your mind around that truth this morning and celebrate it. We have to stop telling God how big our enemies are and begin to say to our enemies how big our God is. Share with the world how much He loves us all, no matter what obstacle we face or the size of our sins.

Romans 5:8-11 tells us this, "But God demonstrated his own love for us in this: While we were still sinners,

Christ died for us. Since we have now been justified by his blood, how much more shall we be saved from God's wrath through him. For if, when we were God's enemies, we were reconciled to him through the death of his Son, how much more, having been reconciled, shall we be saved through his life! Not only is this so, but we also rejoice in God through our Lord Jesus Christ, through whom we have now received reconciliation."

There is nothing that can separate us from the love of Christ. "Thank you, Lord!"

-22-
Preach The Word

I want to share a word of encouragement today that comes from 2 Timothy 4:1-5 which says:

"In the presence of God and of Jesus Christ, who will judge the living and the dead, and in view of his appearing and his kingdom, I give you this charge: Preach the Word; be prepared in season and out of season; correct, rebuke and encourage-with great patience and careful instruction. For the time will come when men will not put up with sound doctrine. Instead, to suit their own desires, they will gather around them a number of teachers to say what their itching ears want to hear. They will turn their ears away from the truth and turn to myths. But you, keep your head in the situations, endure hardship, do the work of an evangelist, discharge all the duties of ministry."

How accurate is God's Word? So many people believe the lies of Satan, and they fall right into his snares. They chase after lies that sound so good to their itching ears. But Paul gives us something we, as believers, need to hang on to! He said, "Preach the Word and be prepared." Are you prepared to preach the Word? Is your life a living testimony of what His amazing grace can do in one's life?

This world needs to hear Truth. This world needs to hear how much God loves them. This world needs to know what it means to be a child of the King. So listen, keep your head in all situations, do the evangelist's work, and serve the Lord with all your heart.

Paul continues to write in 2 Timothy 4:6-8 and says,

"For I am already being poured out like a drink offering, and the time has come for my departure. I have fought the good fight, I have finished the race. I have kept the faith. Now there is in store for me the crown of righteousness, which the Lord, the righteous Judge, will award to me on that day-and not only me but also to all who have longed for his appearing."

Make the most of every opportunity the Lord gives us to share the Good News of Jesus; then, one day, you can repeat these words of Paul. "I have fought the good fight, I have finished the race, I have kept the faith."

-23-

Where's The Passion?

I was sitting in my chair, spending a little time with God, and a wave of concern flooded my mind and heart. What was so strange was that I wasn't concerned for those without Christ; it was those who were believers. Where is the passion among the Church of Jesus Christ? Where is the excitement and joy from their walk with the Father? Where's the drive and the energy that grows as you dive into God's Word? I challenge you, the Church, to dream. There are believers with no dreams. Their lives are marked as being frustrated, bored, and regretful. So many of us have plans, but we dream way too small, so we settle and turn to more self-centered passions. How many of us today are looking back and wondering, what have I done with my life? You are living in regret and wonder what could have been.

I want to encourage you to discover your God-dream for your life. Set down with the Lord, ask Him to show you your gift, and then ask Him how to use that gift to share His love. Then ask yourself three questions: First, is my dream God-honoring? Second, will my dream change people's lives? Third question, do my dreams resonate with godly people?

Do we believe in God for the impossible? Are we full of faith and passion? Are we dreaming God-filled dreams?

Philippians 4:13 says, "I can do all things through Christ who gives me strength."

In Matthew 19:26: Jesus looked at them and said, "With man this is impossible, but with God all things are possible."

Be willing to step out on faith and place your trust in the God of the universe. Let's go, Church! It's time to be the light of the world. We have a message to share that will change the world. We can't be quiet, and we can't sit back and close our eyes. We can't be content and not share the Gospel of Jesus Christ. Dream big, but pray bigger.

~24~

He Is Righteous

I don't know about you, but I must hear some truth today. I'm tired of hearing lies and all the negative stuff happening worldwide. What about you? Do you need something positive? Do you need something that will put a smile on your face? Then get into God's Word.

Psalm 145:17-21 says, "The Lord is righteous in all his ways and loving towards all he has made. The Lord is near to all who call on him, to all who call on him in truth. He fills the desires of those who fear him; he hears their cry and saves them. The Lord watches over all who love him, but all the wicked he will destroy. My mouth will speak praise of the Lord. Let every creature praise his holy name forever and ever."

He is near to all who call out to Him. He hears our cry for help and watches over each day with love. He deserves our praise today. He is righteous, and He loves justice.

Psalm 66;1-5 says, "Shout with joy to God, all the earth. Sing the glory of his name; make his praise glorious! Say to God, 'How awesome are your deeds! So great is your power that your enemies cringe before you. All the earth bows down to you; they sing praise to you, they sing praise to your name.' Come and see what God has done, how awesome he works on man's behalf!"

I encourage you to thank Him for the three blessings that He has given you. Then, after you have written them out, think of ways to use those blessings to bless others.

-25-

Worship

It's time to worship! Psalm 150:6 says this,

"Let everything that has breath praise the Lord."

It's not because we got to, but we get to! You may be going through a tough season in life, and you feel God has forgotten you. You feel like you can't catch a break and feel so weighed down. I don't mean to over-simplify life or belittle your troubles, but God's Word gives us a way to deal with these seasons of life.

> *James 5:13: "Are any of you in trouble? He should pray. Is anyone happy? Let him sing songs of praise."*

> *Psalm 95:6-7: "Come, let us bow down in worship, let us kneel before the Lord our Maker; for he is our God and we are the people of his pasture, the flock under his care."*

> *Psalm 96:1-5: "Sing to the Lord a new song; sing to the Lord, all the earth. Sing to the Lord, praise his name; proclaim his salvation day after day. Declare his glory among the nations, his marvelous deeds among all peoples. For great is the Lord and most worthy of praise; he is to be feared above all gods. For the gods of the nations are idols, but the Lord made the heavens."*

Let's raise the roof and sing praise to the King of kings and the Lord of lords. He is the Creator, the Conquering King, the Risen One, the Alpha, and Omega.

> *Psalm 98:1-5: "Sing to the Lord a new song, for he has done marvelous things; his fight hand and his holy arm have worked salvation for him. The Lord has made his salvation known and revealed his righteousness to the nations. He has remembered his love and his faithfulness to the house of Israel; all the ends of the earth have seen the salvation of our God. Shout for joy to the Lord, all the earth, burst into jubilant song with music; make music to the Lord with the harp, with the harp and the song of singing."*

Let the rivers clap their hands, let the mountains sing together for joy, and let His Church rise up and worship Him. Then see how the worries of this life fade away.

~26~

Losing Air?

Most of our cars ride on four tires. Air pressure varies from car to car, but all four tires must have equal air pressure to perform their best. When one tire's air pressure is low, it will cause issues when you don't correct the situation immediately. I have been guilty of ignoring the low pressure, and I kept making excuses for not stopping to fix the issue. First, I would say, "I don't have time; I will do it tomorrow." Then I would use the same excuse the next day too. Low air pressure and unbalanced tires will cause your car to pull to the right or the left. It will also cause your tires to wear out much faster than expected. That will cost you more money and cause more headaches. Then you start thinking, why didn't I slow down long enough to get the tires right?

Properly balancing and aligning your tires may cost you a little more upfront, but your car will perform much better and last longer. So here is my question for you today, is your life perfectly balanced and aligned with the Lord? Are you growing in wisdom, stature, and favor with God and man? Is there a "tire" that is losing air? Is your life pulling to the right or left? You may be like me, and you must slow down enough to look honestly at your life and your walk with God. Please pay attention to the warning lights of life and do something about it now. Jesus was balanced in every area of life. He is our ultimate example of how to live life. So be willing to follow the example of the Total Package!

> Luke 2:52 says, "Jesus grew in wisdom and stature, and in favor with God and men."

~27~
What Drives You?

It is time to dive into the Word of God. I want to ask you a simple question. What drives your life? Think about it. Everyone is driven by something. What is it? Some people are driven by guilt. They spend their whole life running from regret and bad decisions. They allow their past to control their future. But the good news is that your past does not limit God. I know great men of God in His Word that messed up big time, and He still did excellent work in their lives. He can do the same in your life. Some are driven by resentment and anger. Instead of forgiving and letting things go, we tend to hang on and never dismiss. Resentment always hurts you more than it does the other person. Your past is the past. You are only hurting yourself with your bitterness. Forgive and let it go. It will take a load off of you. Many people are driven by fear. Fear is a liar, and it keeps you from God's best.

> First John 14:18: "There is no fear in love. But perfect love drives out fear because fear has to do with punishment. The one who fears is not made perfect in love."

Embrace God's love through faith in Jesus Christ. God hasn't given us a spirit of fear. Here is a good one. Many of us are driven by materialism—the desire to acquire. We are trying to keep up with the Jones. The sad thing is that possession only provides temporary happiness, and you still must pay for it. Those things we thought would bring us fulfillment and joy will leave us empty. Absolute security can only be found in a loving relationship with Jesus. Finally, the need for approval drives some people. Those who follow the crowd usually get lost in it. One key to failure is to try and please everyone. The opinions of others cannot control us. Nothing matters more than knowing God's purpose for your life. No success, fame, or material thing can replace that. We all get out of whack sooner or later. So many times, our priorities seem to be all out of order. I can't tell you how often I have had to stop and ask myself, " How did I get here?"

> Matthew 6:24 says, "No one can serve two masters. Either he will hate the one and love the other, or he will be devoted to the one and despise the other. You cannot serve both God and money."

The challenge for today: Put God first and let go of the past. Give God your fears and your worldly desires that are driving you. Only He can satisfy and complete you. Start your day with the One who holds it all in place. Minimize the distractions in life and constantly keep your eyes fixed on your Heavenly Father.

~28~
Prepared?

Are you prepared? Are you ready?

Matthew 24:36-44 says, "No one knows about that day or hour, not even the angels in heaven, nor the Son, but only the Father. As it was in the days of Noah, so it will be at the coming of the Son of Man. For in the days before the flood, people will be eating and drinking, marrying and giving in marriage, up to the day Noah entered the ark; and they knew nothing about what would happen until the flood came and took them all away. That is how it will be at the coming of the Son of Man. Two men will be in the field; one will be taken and the other left. Two women will be grinding with a hand mill; one will be taken and the other left. Therefore keep watch, because you do not know on what day your Lord will come. But understand this: If the owner of the house had known at what time of night the thief was coming, he would have kept watch and would not have let his house be broken into. So you also must be ready, because the Son of Man will come at an hour when you do not expect him."

Do you have a personal relationship with Jesus Christ? Are you prepared? Heaven is a ready place for a prepared person. But unfortunately, you can't be good enough, nor can you earn your way to heaven.

John 3:16: "For God so loved the world that he gave his one and only Son, that whoever believes in him shall not perish but have eternal life."

He calls you today to surrender your life, follow Him in obedience, and receive His amazing grace. It will be the most significant decision you will ever make. He is coming again, so make sure that you keep watching.

~29~
Two Things Needed

Jesus shares a truth with us in John 16 that should rock your prayer life. So many times, we sit down with God and break out our want list, ask God for so many things, and then say our Amen. But do we even listen to His response back to us? Do we take time to hear His instructions for the day? There are two things we need so that we can hear our Father's voice in today's world. First, we must have a pure heart. Secondly, we must have a listening ear. We have to take time to stop and listen and not be in a hurry to rush away.

> *John 16:12-15 Jesus tells us this, "I have much more to say to you, more than you can now bear. But when he, the Spirit of truth, comes, he will guide you into all truth. He will not speak on his own; he will speak only what he hears, and he will tell you what is yet to come. He will bring glory to me by taking from mine and making it known to you. All that belongs to the Father is mine. That is why I said the Spirit will take from what is mine and make it known to you."*

That is such a crazy word from Jesus. We should wake up every morning with excitement and joy to discover what Jesus has to say to us today. What is He trying to tell you today? The Savior of the world wants to share a word with you today. Will you stop long enough to listen?

Take time to evaluate your prayer life, and ask the Lord what you must do, or confess to having that pure heart. You may be surprised by what He may show you. Don't run off in fear or embarrassment; receive it with love. Then ask God to show you how to free up time and rearrange your schedule. It may involve resetting your priorities and cutting out some good things to make room for the best. I pray that your prayer life grows and that you will see the power of God working in your life.

~30~
The Word

I want to encourage you all to spend time in God's Word. Please don't rush through it to check a box; slow down and let it go deep. Then, ask the Lord how you can apply this truth to your life.

> Deuteronomy 6:6-9 says, "These commands I give you today are to be upon your hearts. Impress them on your children. Talk about them when you sit at home and when you walk along the road, when you lie down and when you get up. Tie them as a symbol on your hands and bind them on your foreheads. Write them on the doorframes of your houses and on your gates."

I love the old saying I have written in my Bible, which goes like this: "Sin will keep you from this Book, or this Book will keep you from sin." How true is that? Be careful not to forget the Lord and the powerful Word of God. Set aside time each day to take in God's Word, then find a way to give it away. It will create a continual flow of the power of the Holy Spirit in your life and the life of the Church.

~31~
Pride

Proverbs 6:16-19 says, "There are six things the Lord hates, seven that are detestable to him: Proud look, a lying tongue, and hands that shed innocent blood, a heart that devises wicked schemes, feet that are quick to rush into evil, false witness who pours out lies, and a man who stirs up dissension among the brothers."

If that is what God hates, we will do well to avoid all those things. But look what tops the list, a proud look.

Proverbs 11:2: "When pride comes, then comes disgrace, but with humility comes wisdom."

Proverbs 16:18-19 gives us more truth, "Pride goes before destruction, a haughty spirit before a fall. Better to be lowly in spirit and among the oppressed than to share plunder with the proud."

Proverbs 21:4: "Haughty eyes and a proud heart, the lamp of the wicked, are sin."

Proverbs 13:10: "Pride only breeds quarrels, but wisdom is found in those who take advice."

Are you walking in pride today? Is there a bad attitude that you need to get right before God? What relationship do you need to make right today? Today's the day to swallow pride, pick up the phone and say, "I love you." Let go of the hurt, let go of the pain, let go of the argument that says you were right. It's time to walk in freedom and honor God in every relationship. Whose face did God place in front of you today? Now it's time to walk in obedience. Drop the pride and listen to some good advice from God's Word. Jesus told his disciples in Mark 9:35 and said:

> *"If anyone wants to be first, he must be the very last and the servant of all." Pride has to go.*

Look what Matthew 5:23-24 tells us about pride and our relationships,

> *"Therefore, if you are offering your gift at the altar and there remember that your brother has something against you, leave your gift there in front of the altar. First go and be reconciled to your brother; then come and offer your gift."*

Settle matters quickly, don't allow pride to push it off.

-32-
Truth

I want to share God's Word of encouragement with you before you begin your day. Please take it in, and roll it around in your mind and soul. Chew it over and over again, then swallow. Let it go deep today, and ask God what this means for your life.

> *Ephesians 4:29-33 says, "Do not let any unwholesome talk come out of your mouths, but only what is helpful for the building up according to their needs, that it may benefit those who listen. And do not grieve the Holy Spirit of God, with whom you were sealed for the day of redemption. Get rid of ALL bitterness, rage, and anger, brawling and slander, along with every form of malice. Be kind and compassionate to one another, forgiving each other, just as in Christ God forgave you."*

Where do we even begin? Those verses are jammed packed with godly instructions for our lives. Let's start by asking ourselves some difficult questions like, do my words edify others, or do they tear them down? Am I known as an encourager or a person who is always negative? It is never easy to take an honest look at one's life, but we all must stop and evaluate occasionally. Paul gave us strong words to eliminate bitterness, rage, anger, brawling, and slander. But he also encouraged us to be compassionate and forgiving towards others. Think about it, what has Christ forgiven you for? Has He shown you grace and mercy over the years? We have a call to pursue holiness and follow Jesus' lead in living.

What has God placed in front of you today? What seemed to jump off the page and whisper to your heart? Swallow His truth and let it do its work.

-33-

What Is Needed

In a world full of depression and negativity, how can the Church win? We have to stay encouraged and full of hope! There are five things we need to overcome and defeat the schemes of Satan. First, *"invest in your spiritual growth."* Who is your mentor, and do you have accountability? The second thing we need is to *"understand the power of worship."* Authentic worship renews your strength, reconnects us to God, restores your perspective, rekindles hope, and restores joy in our lives. The third thing we need to do *"is to unleash God's Word in our lives."* Let the Word of God come alive. Begin to ask God daily for wisdom and insight. Put that phone down and turn off the tv and tune into Truth. The fourth supply line to new hope is to *"build great relationships."* In our culture, loneliness is rampant. We all need someone to cheer us on. We all need someone in our corner to give us good advice, fix our cuts, and teach us how to fight. Lastly, *"pay attention to whose voice you are listening to."*

> *James 12:1-2 says, "Therefore, I urge you, brothers, in view of God's mercy, to offer your bodies as a living sacrifice, holy and pleasing to God-this is your spiritual act of worship. Do not conform any longer to the patterns of this world, but be transformed by the renewing of your mind. Then you will be able to test and approve what God's will is-his good, pleasing, and perfect will."*

What voice has your attention? Stay connected to the Father. Church, it is time to fight and win. We don't have time to feel sorry for ourselves or to lick our wounds because there's a world that needs to know about Jesus. Listen, we are on the winning team, and it is time to march out and claim victory in Jesus Christ. Hope is found in a personal relationship with Jesus Christ. Stay connected and receive hope.

~34~

Game Time

Psalm 96:1-4: "Sing to the Lord a new song: sing to the Lord, all the earth. Sing to the Lord, praise his name; proclaim his salvation day after day. Declare his glory among the nations, his marvelous deeds among all peoples. For great is the Lord and most worthy of praise; he is to be feared above all gods."

Athletes warm up before the game and get prepared to play. They not only get their physical bodies ready, but they also train their mind and soul. It's all about the preparation. Church, it's game time! It's time to get out of bed, get that cup of coffee, fuel up, and shower. Then prepare your mind and soul to worship the King of kings today! Break out of that funk of laziness and contentment. Let's worship and honor the Living God with passion and enthusiasm. He deserves our best.

Psalm 66:1-5 says, "Shout with joy to God, all the earth! Sing the glory of his name; make his praise glorious! Say to God, "How awesome are your deeds! So great is your power that your enemies cringe before you. All the earth bows down to you; they sing praise to you, they sing praise to your name." Come and see what God has done, how awesome he works on man's behalf."

Take a look at what David said in Psalm 68:1-4:

"May God arise, may his enemies be scattered; may his foes flee before him. As smoke is blown away by the wind, may you blow them away; as wax melts before the fire, may the wicked perish before God. But may the righteous be glad and rejoice before God; may they be happy and joyful. Sing to God, sing praise to his name, extol him who rides on the clouds."

Let's worship Him today. Let us praise Him with everything we have. Shout to the Lord, the joy of our salvation. Then, let's prepare for our day by spending time with the God of the universe. Amen.

-35-

Be Refreshed

If you need refreshing today, take some time to spend in God's Word. As you read, ask the Lord to give you understanding and wisdom. It is so important to block out time each day to fuel up on God's goodness and strength. I want to share a quick word from Jeremiah, and I pray that you can receive a small treasure from God today.

> *Jeremiah 17:5-6 says, "This is what the Lord says: 'Cursed is the one who trusts in man, who depends on flesh for his strength and whose heart turns away from the Lord. He will be like a bush in the wastelands; he will not see prosperity when it comes. He will dwell in the parched place of the desert, in a salt land where no one lives.'"*

Following after man and trusting in our wisdom doesn't paint a pretty picture. Now take a look at Jeremiah 17:7-8 which says,

> *"But blessed is the man who trusts in the Lord whose confidence is in Him. He will be like a tree planted by the water that sends out its roots by the stream. It does not fear when heat comes; its leaves are always green. It has no worries in a year of drought and never fails to bear fruit."*

Now that describes the kind of life I want to live. How about you? What life do you choose today?

Sit Down At His Table

> *Jeremiah 17:10 tells us, "I the Lord search the heart and examine the mind, to reward a man according to his conduct, according to what his deeds deserve."*

As God searches your heart and examines your mind today, what does He see? Choose today to walk in the presence and goodness of God! The blessed life! Can I get an amen today? God bless you today.

69

~36~

How's The Walk?

Deuteronomy 30:15-16 tells us this, "I set before you today life and prosperity, death and destruction. For I command you today to love the Lord your God, to walk in His ways, and to keep His commands, decrees and laws; then you will live and increase, and the Lord your God will bless you in the land you are entering to possess."

Did you notice the command given by God? He didn't give us an option; He didn't say to pick and choose what we would like to do and do what is convenient for us. Instead, he said, "Love the Lord your God, walk in His ways, and keep His commands." Then He followed it up with a promise: "If you love me and are obedient, I will bless you." Unfortunately, too many professing believers want a buffet-style faith where they can pick and choose what they like and what is easy.

Jesus spoke in Matthew 16:24-25 and said, "If anyone would come after me, he must deny himself and take up his cross and follow me. For whoever wants to save his life will lose it, but whoever loses his life for me will find it."

Following Jesus isn't always easy. There is a cost to becoming a disciple of Christ. Did Jesus live a trouble-free life away from hard times or difficult situations? Certainly not.

Sit Down At His Table

Are you walking out your faith today in a way that pleases God? Are you obeying the call on your life that will make God smile? Do you have peace of knowing that you are dead center in the will of God? Take time to have a one-on-one conversation with your Heavenly Father, and ask Him if He is pleased with your heart. Then patiently sit and wait for His response.

-37-
He's Calling

What has God placed in front of you today? What has God put into you that needs to be released? What is your purpose? In Jeremiah 1:4-5 the Lord speaks to Jeremiah and says,

> *"Before I formed you in the womb I knew you, before you were born I set you apart; I appointed you as a prophet to the nations."*

Wouldn't that be an excellent word from the Lord? Wouldn't you love to hear those words from the Creator God that He has given you a specific job to do? But look at Jeremiah 1:6:

> *"Ah, Sovereign Lord," I said, "I do not know how to speak; I am only a child."*

How often have we made excuses for not following through with what God has called us to do? So many times, God calls us to do something beyond our ability, and we must come to a point where we must trust Him.

> *Jeremiah 1:7-10 the Lord speaks to Jeremiah and says, "Do not say, "I am only a child. You must go to everyone I command you to and say whatever I command you. Do not be afraid of them, for I am with you and will rescue you," declares the Lord. Then the Lord reached out His hand and touched my mouth*

and said to me, "Now, I have put my words in your mouth. See, today I appointed you over nations and kingdoms to uproot and tear down, to destroy and overthrow, to build and to plant."

Do you think Jeremiah was overwhelmed? Do you think Jeremiah had to raise his trust level in God? Look at Jeremiah 1:17, which says this:

"Get yourself ready! Stand up and say to them whatever I command you."

That's a word we need to hold on to today. Get ready, believers in Christ. Prepare your heart, soul, and mind for battle. Stand up for the Word of God and stand up for Truth. Be ready, Church, to say what God has placed in you today. Can you relate to Jeremiah today? Do you understand the fear that Jeremiah faced? Overcome your fear, trust Him fully, and He will fight for you.

-38-

He Is With Us

I don't know about you, but I love some good grilled chicken pulled right off the grill. Set it on a plate with a big baked potato covered in butter, and top it off with some fresh green beans. Man, it is time to eat. In the physical world, that may make your mouth water and may change your meal prep for tonight. But I want to give you some words you must chew on today. I want to encourage you to receive this message of hope for your life today.

The last two years have been crazy. So many people have faced tough times, times of isolation, times of heartache, times of depression, and sorrow. Yet, in all that chaos, God still cares about you and sends hope and peace to His people.

> *Listen to what Isaiah says in Isaiah 40:28-31, "The Lord is the everlasting God, the Creator of the ends of the earth. He will not grow tired or weary, and his understanding no one can fathom. He gives strength to the weary and increases the power of the weak. Even youths grow tired and weary, and young men stumble and fall: but those who hope in the Lord will renew their strength. They will soar on wings like eagles; they will run and not grow weary, they will walk and not faint."*

This is some spiritual food we all need during these crazy times. He is our forever God, the God of endless strength and power, who dishes out hope every day of the week. Because of this truth, we can read Isaiah 41:10 with great confidence:

> *"So do not fear, for I am with you: do not be dismayed, for I am your God. I will strengthen and help you; I will uphold you with my righteous right hand."*

How about that spiritual meal today? Let's eat, church!

-39-

A New Creation

I don't have a story to share or some clever thoughts today. But I do have a powerful scripture to share. Second Corinthians 5:17-21 tells us this:

"If anyone is in Christ, he is a new creation; the old has gone, the new has come! All this is from God, who reconciled us to himself through Christ and gave us the ministry of reconciliation: that God was reconciling the world to himself now Christ, not counting men's sins against them. And he committed to us the message of reconciliation. We are therefore Christ's ambassadors, as though God were making his appeal through us. We implore you on Christ's behalf: Be reconciled to God. God made him who had no sin to be sin for us, so that in him we might become the righteousness of God."

Reading this scripture should change the way we live our life today. It should affect that negative attitude you have been hanging on to for weeks.

Take your eyes off yourself today and turn them to the truth. In Christ, you have a new beginning; you are loved and adored by the Creator of the universe. Because of what Christ has done for us, we are made right before God Himself.

There is nothing we have done to deserve this, but it's only because of His amazing grace! Church, can we thank

Him today? Can we offer up praise for this blessing? "Thank you, Lord, for the gift of King Jesus."

-40-

A Pop In The Belly

More than ever, "believers" in today's church find many reasons not to attend corporate worship. I don't want to be negative, but sometimes you must speak the truth. Yesterday, Laura and I were driving back from Atlanta, and it was a long 8-hour drive. Most of our time was spent on I-75, and I was getting sleepy. I tried chewing gum, rolling down the wind, and turning up the music. Nothing seemed to work. I would be fine if I could close my eyes for a second. As my eyes closed, Laura popped me in the belly and said, "We need to pull over!" It ticked me off; I didn't want to stop, we had to get home, and I certainly didn't like her popping me in the belly! Guess what we did? We pulled over at a coffee shop, walked around, went to the restrooms, and got their largest coffee. We made it back safe and sound.

Oh, how the Church of Jesus Christ needs a pop in the belly. We need to wake up from the mundane spiritual gazing that causes us to drift off to sleep spiritually. I know you have places and people to see, but sometimes it's best to pull over and wake yourself up.

Jesus said in Revelation 2:4-5, "Yet I hold this against you: You have forsaken your first love. Remember the height from which you have fallen. Repent and do the things you did at first."

Lord, wake us up from our spiritual slumber! Lord, pop us in the belly if that's what it takes. Help us to turn our eyes and heart back to you. To You be the glory and honor today.

-41-

Let Go

I want to ask you two simple questions today, and I was hoping you could think through them before you answer. First question: Is there something you need to let go of **today**? Second question: is there something you're holding on to out of fear, not faith?

> *Matthew 10:39 says, "Whoever finds their life will lose it, and whoever loses their life for my sake will find it."*

Maybe it's time to let go of your time, talent, and treasure and see what God can do with it.

Fear is a liar, and Satan uses fear to rob us of our joy daily. Satan reminds you of your past sins, failures, and shortcomings. He loves to bring up your past and remind you of how dirty your thought life was and how selfish you could be regarding friendships. He loves to cover you with guilt and shame and will try to push you away from God. Let go of your past sins and failures.

> *1 John 1:9: "If we confess our sins, he is faithful and just and will forgive us our sins and purify us from all unrighteousness."*

Know that if you are in Christ, you have been restored and set free through the blood of Jesus Christ. Stomp out the lies of Satan and confront them with the truth. If you are a child of God, you are forgiven, and the King of kings loves you. Once you are free of guilt and shame, you can dream in Jesus Christ. The time and energy you once spent worrying and thinking about the past can now be used to develop your gift and love for the Lord. Let go of your gift and trust God with it. Be open to stepping up even when you feel way over your head. Jump into the harness of Christ and yoke up with the Father.

> *Matthew 11:29-30: "Take my yoke upon you and learn of me, for I am gentle and humble in heart, and you will find rest for your souls. For my yoke is easy and my burden is light."*

What is God saying to you this morning? It's time to stop making excuses and do what God has equipped and called you to be. Let go of your past and begin to dream in Christ Jesus. He will help carry the load.

-42-

Are You Ready For Good News?

Who wants to hear some good news? Who in this world wants to listen to a positive message? Who in this world today needs to be encouraged? If you are like me, I am tired of hearing the world's noise, the lies of Satan, and seeing so many people living in fear. I need God's Word; how about you? I am so tired of turning on the news; all I hear is what is wrong with this world. Everything that makes the headlines is murders, scandals, or devasting news.

Get ready to receive some good news this morning from First John 5:1-5:

> "Everyone who believes that Jesus is the Christ is born of God, and everyone who loves the Father loves his child as well. This is how we know that we live the children of God: by loving God and carrying out his commands. This is love for God: to obey His commands. And his commands are not burdensome, for everyone born of God overcomes the world. This is the victory that has overcome the world, even our faith. Who is it that overcomes the world? Only he who believes that Jesus is the Son of God."

Now that is good news! That is what the Church of Jesus Christ should be talking about and proclaiming to the world. Listen, if you are in Christ, you are an overcomer and can live a life full of happiness, peace, and joy. Today is the day the Lord has made; let's live it up and make it count for the glory of God.

If that wasn't enough, here is more good news that is found in Romans 8:1-2 which says this:

> *"Therefore, there is no condemnation for those who are in Christ Jesus, because through Christ Jesus the law of the Spirit of life set me free from the law of sin and death."*

We can experience victory over sin and death because of what Jesus Christ did for us on Calvary. He was buried in a tomb but arose from the grave and is alive and well today. So let's celebrate this fantastic news with the rest of the world.

-43-

Tired Of Walking The Hills?

Laura and I walk our dog Miles every day. We have two different routes we can take on any given day. Yesterday we chose the shorter route and walked through our neighborhood. At the end of the route, Laura decides not to head to the house but to take a left and walk up this huge hill. The first thing that came out of my mouth was, "I am not going to walk up that hill; I am tired." So guess who walked up that hill with Miles and Laura? I complained up that hill and couldn't wait to return to level ground!

Psalm 143:8-10: "Let the morning bring me word of your unfailing love, for I have put trust in you. Show me the way I should go, for to you I lift up my soul. Rescue me from my enemies, O Lord, for I hide myself in you. Teach me to do your will, for you are my God; may your Spirit lead me to level ground."

Do you need to get back on level ground today? Has the hill of life beaten you down? Ask God today to give you directions and understanding. Ask Him to rescue you, hide in His goodness, and enjoy His presence. Hills in life usually make us whine and complain but also strengthen us. So I pray today that God will lead you back to level ground, but don't forget to appreciate the climb.

-44-

Praying With Power

There have been a couple of times when I have struggled in my prayer life. I would love to tell you that my prayer life is amazing and one of the most exciting things, but I would be lying to you. If you lack or struggle in your prayer life, I encourage you to write your prayers to the Lord. I don't know about you, but it helps me to stay focused and on point with the Lord. The second thing I want to encourage you to do is to pray the scriptures.

> *Ephesians 1:17-21: "I keep asking that God, our Father, may give you the Spirit of wisdom and revelation, so that you may know Him better. I pray also that the eyes of your heart may be enlightened in order that the hope to which He has called you, the riches of his glorious inheritance in the saints, and his incomparably great power do for us who believe. That power is the working of his mighty strength, which he exerted in Christ when he raised him from the dead and seated him at his right hand in the heavenly realms, far above all rule and authority, power, and dominion, and every title that has been given, not only in the present age but also in the one to come."*

I want to challenge you today to make this prayer in Ephesians personal and put it in your own words, then watch your prayer life come alive. Lord, send your miracle-working power today. Don't be scared to switch things up regarding your prayer time, and be open to talking with other godly leaders you respect about your personal prayer time with the Lord.

~45~

Dare To Dream

Dare to dream today; if you are in Christ, dream big! Because we serve a huge and mighty God. But you can't be scared to get your feet wet. God performed a huge miracle in Joshua 3 when he parted the Jordan River.

> Let's read together Joshua 3:5-8, "Joshua told the people, "Consecrate yourselves, for tomorrow the Lord will do amazing things among you." Joshua said to the priest, "Take up the ark of the covenant and pass on ahead of the people." So they took it up and went ahead of them. And the Lord said to Joshua, "Today I will begin to exalt you in the eyes of all Israel, so that they may know that I am with you as I was with Moses. Tell the priests who carry the ark of the covenant: 'When you reach edge of the Jordan's water, go and stand in the river.'"

Here is the challenge for us today. Set yourself apart, dive deep into God's Word, and take time to hear the voice of the Lord. When you hear a word from the Lord, pay attention to His details, and obey His every word. But to see your Jordan River parted, you must get your feet wet first. Here is where many God dreams stall out. We are waiting for God to do His part while God is waiting for us to step into the water. It will require faith! You are one decision away from a different life in Christ. If you can take that first step, He will take it from there. What has God placed in your heart? What's holding you back from what God has called you to do? What fear have you paralyzed standing on the shore?

Today is the day to get your feet wet, trust Him fully, and chase your calling and passion. So enjoy your worship time today.

-46-
Count Your Blessings

Have you ever felt like God has forgotten you? Has your focus turned to all the negativity around you?

> *Psalm 77:4-9: "You keep my eyes from closing; I was too troubled to speak. I thought about the former days, the years so long ago; I remembered my songs in the night. My heart muses and my spirit inquired: 'Will the Lord reject forever? Will He never show His favor again? Has his unfailing love vanished forever? Has God forgotten to be merciful? Has He in anger withheld his compassion?'"*

Have you ever had some of those sleepless nights or some of those difficult days when you seemed so defeated and overwhelmed? Then pause for just a few minutes and sit back and see what the writer of Psalm 77 says next.

> *Psalm 77:11-15 he writes, "I will remember the deeds of the Lord; yes, I will remember your miracles of long ago. I will meditate on all your works and consider all your mighty deeds. Your ways, O God, are holy. What god is so great as our God? You are the God who performs miracles; you display your power among your people. With your mighty arm you redeem your people."*

When we are in the dumps of life, we start counting the blessings God gave us in the past. If you want a good night's sleep, don't count sheep. Count blessings. Gratitude improves the quality of life. Count your blessings; name them one by one. I dare you to try it.

-47-
God Is Good

Psalm 34:8: "Taste and see that the Lord is good; blessed is the man who takes refuge in Him."

In this life, we will all have heartache and pain. We will all face difficult situations and brutal seasons in life. There will be times when we feel alone, depressed, defeated, or overwhelmed. When the storms of life come, it seems like they will never end. I want to encourage you today to hold on, don't give up, and hold on to the truth! Take your focus off the difficulty. Take your focus off the sickness. Take your focus off the hard times and turn your attention to the very One who created you.

When you are worried, then worship the Lord. When you are depressed, then worship the Lord. When you are overwhelmed, then worship the Lord.

Psalm 34:17-19: "The righteous cry out, and the Lord hears them; he delivers them from all their troubles. The Lord is near the brokenhearted and saves those who are crushed in spirit. A righteous man may have many troubles, but the Lord delivers him from them all."

Our Redeemer is faithful and true. Who can testify today? God is good, and He is good all the time.

-48-

God Is Love

So many people who reject God aren't rejecting God but leaving religion without knowing it. If you don't love God, you don't know God. It would be impossible to resist His unconditional, never-ending love. God is love, and nothing can separate us from it. There is nothing you can do to make Him love you any less.

First John 4:16-19 tells us this, "And so we know and rely on the love God has for us. God is love. Whoever lives in love, lives in God, and God in him. In this way, love is made complete among us so that we will have confidence on the day of judgment, because in this world we are like him. There is no fear in love. But perfect love drives out fear, because fear has to do with punishment. The one who fears is not made perfect in love. We love, because He first loved us."

First John 5:1-5: "Everyone who believes that Jesus is the Christ is born of God, and everyone who loves the father loves his child as well. This is how we know that we love the children of God: by loving God and carrying out his commands. This is love for God: to obey his commands. And his commands are not burdensome, for everyone born of God overcomes the world. This is the victory that has overcome the world, even our faith. Who is it that overcomes the world? Only he who believes that Jesus is the Son of God."

"Thank you, Lord, for your love." Let's celebrate His unconditional love today.

-49-
Self Or Christ

We live in a day when the things of God are not high on our priority list. I am not talking about unbelievers; I am talking about the Church. I am talking about those who have surrendered their lives to Jesus Christ and professed Him as Lord and Savior. I can be so selfish. I want to encourage you today to slow down long enough to take inventory of what you hold dear and ask yourself, what am I living for? Here is another way to ask: Whom are you living for? Self or Christ?

Romans 8:5-8 tells us, "Those who live according to the sinful nature have their minds set on what that nature desires; but those who live in accordance with the Spirit have their minds set on what the Spirit desires. The mind of the sinful man is death, but the mind controlled by the Spirit is life and peace. The sinful mind is hostile to God. It does not submit to God's law, nor can it do so. Those controlled by the sinful nature cannot please God."

I want to pray over you a blessing today found in Numbers 6:24-26:

"The Lord bless you and keep you; the Lord make his face shine upon you and be gracious to you; the Lord turn his face towards you and give you peace."

Yes, I pray God's best for you today and that you can receive this truth. But know this; God doesn't bless you to raise your standard of living. God will bless us to increase our standard of giving. Receive it today so you can give it away. Keep your eyes wide open today.

-50-

Pray Big

I am blessed to live in Titusville, Florida, fifteen minutes from the beach. Many mornings, I love to get up and watch the sunrise in the East sky over the ocean. Somedays, it will take your breath away. As I sit and look at God's handiwork, I get lost in His love and power! I love sitting here thinking about how He spoke everything into existence and placed life into man. But how many times do we take His love for granted? How many times do we take His power for granted? How often do we not honor Him with our life or ministry when we do things in our strength and dream too small? How many of us today are walking in the same old rut you traveled for 20 years with God? You find comfort in that rut because it is easy, and you don't have to trust God. You are stuck spiritually.

It's time to dig a new trench or push out from the shore. In Luke 5, the disciples stood by the Lake of Gennesaret, washing their nets. They fished all night, but they caught nothing. Instead, there was a crowd around Jesus listening to his every word. Jesus needed a little space so all the people could hear. So Jesus jumped into Simon's boat and asked him to push out from the shore, and Jesus began to teach God's Word.

After Jesus was finished teaching, he said to Simon in Luke 5:4:

> *"Put out into deep water, and let down the nets for a catch."*

It didn't make sense to Simon to push out to deep water; I never caught anything in deep water. Plus, I just washed my nets, and it's not even the right time of day to catch fish. But Simon listened to Jesus, did precisely what Jesus told him, and brought in the biggest fish he had ever seen.

If you are struggling in your walk with Christ and you feel as if you are in a giant spiritual rut, I challenge you today to change your prayer life and start praying bold prayers. This challenge may not make much sense to you, but here you are, struggling spiritually and asking me to pray boldly. It's time to push away from the shore of faith. You see, God honors bold prayers because bold prayers praise God. So dare to dream today for the glory of God. Overcome your fears, get off the spiritual bank, and push into the deep water. Pray Big! Pray boldly. He is waiting for the prayer warriors to up their game.

-51-
Fight Back

How often have you messed up or fallen short of what God has called you to be? How many times have we tripped up in Satan's snares of life? Are you overwhelmed with discouragement or just stuck in doing life? Satan wants you to be focused on the negative things of this world; he loves to get you covered up with your past failures. He wants to overwhelm you with lies about your body, friendships, and personal life. He is in full attack mode, and he wants to destroy you. I challenge you to fill your mind with the Word of God. Fight back, don't let him keep blasting you with things that are not true. Say no to his lies, stand today, and be the aggressor.

Then take time to meditate on Romans 4:7-8:

"Blessed are they whose transgressions are forgiven, whose sins are covered. Blessed is the man whose sin the Lord will never count against him."

If you are in Christ, you are forgiven, your sins have been paid for, and you have been set free! You are a child of the King, and your Heavenly Father greatly loves you. So, take that in, roll it around in your mind, and receive that good word. Turn to the positive and the Word of God. Because of what Jesus has done for us, we are blessed. Say that over and over again in your head. We are blessed! We are blessed! We are blessed!

Ephesians 6:10-13: "Finally be strong in the Lord and in his mighty power. Put on the full armor of God so that you can take your stand against the devil's schemes. For our struggle is not against flesh and blood, but against the rulers, against the authorities, against the power of this dark world and against the spiritual forces of evil in heavenly realms. Therefore put on the full armor of God, so that when the day of evil comes, you may be able to stand your ground."

Today, don't allow Satan to feed you lies and cause you discouragement. But stand on God's truth and receive the hope that only comes from your walk with Jesus Christ. Don't give in, don't back down, and keep fighting.

~52~
Under Attack?

Psalm 56:1-4: "Be merciful to me, O God, for men hotly pursue me; all day long they press their attack. My slanderers pursue me all day long; many are attacking me in their pride. When I am afraid, I will trust in you. In God, whose word I praise, in God I trust, I will not be afraid. What can a mortal man do to me?"

David also wrote Psalm 25:19-20: "See how my enemies have increased and how fiercely they hate me! Guard my life and rescue me; let me not be put to shame, for I take refuge in you."

At some time or another, we all have experienced the attacks of Satan. If you run after the Lord and try to serve Him, you will face obstacles, roadblocks, and people who will slander you. It's all a part of the spiritual war we fight, but just like David, take refuge in God.

I encourage you today to keep pressing forward and keep your eyes on Jesus. But also ask yourself, who do you lean on when things don't go your way? Who do you put your trust in when your plans begin to unravel? I pray you can speak the words of David and say, "In God I trust, I will not be afraid." Place your trust in the One who hung the moon and the stars. He never fails and loves you more than you will ever know.

~53~
Reflect His Grace

Thought for today: Jesus accepted people blinded by sin, those who disagreed with him, those who let him down, and those who criticized him. Jesus valued everyone.

> *Matthew 9:35-36: "Jesus went through all the towns and villages, teaching in their synagogues, preaching the good news of the kingdom and healing every disease and sickness. When he saw the crowds, he had compassion on them, because they were harassed and helpless, like a sheep without a shepherd.*

Jesus didn't judge people based on their appearance or how much money they made, but he truly loved them. So Paul writes in Romans 14:1-4 and says:

> *"Accept him whose faith is weak, without passing judgment on disputable matters. One man's faith allows him to eat everything, but another man, whose faith is weak, eats only vegetables. The man who eats everything must not look down on those who do not, and the man who does not eat everything must not condemn the man who does, for God has accepted him. Who are you to judge someone else's servant?"*

When we accept only those who love or think like us, we do no more than people who do not know God! Accept the weak in faith. Don't pass judgment; it's not our job. We can't stick our noses in the air and think we are better than someone struggling with sin. Think about this, how did Christ receive you? He accepted you just like you were, with all your faults, issues, and mess-ups. He didn't say, "Change to be like me, and then I accept you." He said, "Come as you are!"

Look at what Paul wrote in Romans 5:8, "But God demonstrates his own love for us in this: While we were still sinners, Christ died for us."

While we were still dirty and covered in sin, He showed us grace! When our mind was polluted with worldly trash, He still loved and forgave me. "Thank the Lord today for His amazing grace." Can we begin to see people with the eyes of Christ? Can we begin to love others and not pass judgment. Extend His grace to others today, even in Walmart.

-54-
Staying Pure

How can we keep our ways pure as believers in Jesus Christ? That is the question we need to be able to answer. Temptation has existed since Adam and Eve, but evil is greatly intensifying today. Second Timothy says, "Evil men and impostors will go from bad to worse, deceiving and being deceived." Back in the day, a man had to go to a curb store to pick up what I called a 'dirty book,' He had to ask the clerk for it because it was behind the front counter. Nowadays, the world of pornography is sitting right there on your cell phone. A device that you carry around with you everywhere you go. We are all guilty of looking at or seeing things on our phones that don't please God. It's hard not to get down on yourself or feel guilty when things happen without warning. All the great people of God faced temptation, and many fell and fell hard. Satan uses some of the same tricks as he did in the days of David when he fell into lust, greed, and deception. He is very good at making evil look good until it bites you like a serpent.

So again, how can we keep our ways pure?

Psalm 119:9-16: "By living according to your word. I seek you with all my heart; do let me stray from your commands. I have hidden your word in my heart that I might not sin against you. Praise be to you, O Lord; teach me your decrees. With my lips I recount all the laws that come from your mouth. I rejoice in following your statues as one rejoices in great riches. I meditate on your precepts and consider your ways. I delight in your decrees; I will not neglect your word."

I encourage you to become a student of the Word and always to keep it in front of you. This commitment may be demanding, but I challenge you to spend more time in God's Word than on your phone. Fight the good fight, stay in God's Word, and He will direct your path. He will help you to make good decisions, and His Word will bring you victory, and it will give you everything you need to overcome the schemes of the slithering serpent. So walk in victory today, and dive deep into His Word.

-55-
More Than You Can Handle

Have you ever heard someone say, "God will never give you more than you can handle?" While this sounds spiritual, nowhere in the Bible does it say that.

> *First Corinthians 10:13 does say, "God is faithful; he will not let you be tempted beyond what you can bear."*

But scripture never says that God won't give you more than you can handle. Through my experiences as a minister of the Lord, God often allows me to experience more than I can take to teach me to trust and depend on Him. In Second Corinthians, Paul had what he called a "thorn in the flesh." Some scholars say he had trouble seeing as a result of his Damascus experience with the Lord in Acts chapter nine. We also know that Paul pleaded with God to take this "thorn in the flesh" away, but God never did. Rather than allowing this "thorn in the flesh" to turn him away from God, Paul decided to trust God and let it pull him closer. During the struggle, God spoke to Paul and offered him this promise in Second Corinthians 12:9-10:

> *"My grace is sufficient for you, for my power is made perfect in weakness." Therefore I will boast all the more gladly about my weakness, so that Christ's power may rest on me. That is why, for Christ sake, I delight in weakness, in insults, in hardships, in*

persecutions, in difficulties. For when I am weak, then I am strong."

God's presence was all Paul needed.

Today's challenge is this: never be afraid to move forward through a challenge, a storm in life, or a trail in front of you because it feels like more than you can handle. We are always tempted to put on a show and say, "I got this; I need to be strong." But the truth is it's okay to be weak. For when I am weak, He is strong. God will use our "thorns in the flesh" to change us into the image of His Son and teach us to trust Him. Then, somehow or someway, God will use that trial as a vehicle for a blessing. So be encouraged today; God is good.

~56~

I Can't Carry It No Further

I had this big tree outside my back door that blocked the sun from shining and stopped the grass from growing. It also dropped leaves and sticks continuously on my small patio, and I could never keep it clean. Plus, this tree was a haven for squirrels that drove my dog crazy. So my wife and I decided this tree had to go. I could cut this tree down, but it was only twenty feet from the house, so I needed someone who knew what they were doing. My friend Matt was ripping out my old carpet and replacing it with some beautiful new wood planks, and he heard my wife and me. It's a conversation about cutting down the tree at our backdoor. Matt looked at us and said, "I can cut that tree down for you with no problem, matter of fact, I can do it tomorrow."

The next day, Matt shows up with a ladder, a chainsaw, and a rope. He knew exactly what to cut first and where each limb would fall, and he had that big tree down in three hours. Now the job was to cut that tree into smaller pieces and somehow get it to the front yard by the street. Thank goodness he brought some hand trucks to help with this crazy tree. We grunted, pulled, pushed, and finally managed to get everything to the road, and now I was hoping the city would pick it up because I couldn't carry it any further. I was exhausted; I was worn out. That headache of a tree sat on the road for days, and the neighbors were getting frustrated; it was an eyesore. My wife finally called the city and asked if they could come by and get all the debris off the roadside. The next day, they brought a truck with a lift, and within a few minutes, every limb and heavy piece of wood was removed.

What are you carrying today that is weighing you down? Is there something you are facing, and you need help with what direction to go or how to handle the situation? I encourage you to have the courage to ask for help and not be scared to share your burden with a trusted friend. Sooner or later, we all need help! For some, it's a sin or a burden that you have been carrying for years, and you can't get it to your front yard in an attempt to haul it off, and you can't take it any further.

Here is the good news today First John 1:9 says:

> *"If we confess our sins, he is faithful and just and will forgive us our sins and purify us from all unrighteousness."*

Yes! If you call, He will haul it all off. Rest in His love and grace today.

-57-
The Battle of the Mind

Do you like the direction your thoughts are taking you? Proverbs 23:7 tell us this:

"For as he thinks in his heart, so is he."

The life we have reflects what we think. I don't know where you are today or what is going on in your mind. But I can tell you this, with God's help, you can transform your mind and change your entire world. You can allow God to renew your mind by filling you with His unchanging truth.

First, you must identify what is holding your mind captive. What is trapping you from enjoying God's goodness and the joy of life? What lie have you bought into that runs through your mind repeatedly? I may be oversimplifying things but remove the lie. Your mind is a war zone, and you are under attack.

John 10:10: "The thief comes to kill, steal, and destroy."

You have to know that you are in an all-out war. You cannot change what you do not confront. Satan loves to plant seeds of doubt, confusion, worry, and anxiety. He loves robbing you of joy, peace, and happiness. The enemy wants to strip you of all fulfillment and knowing you are so loved. He is the father of lies, the great deceiver, and your enemy.

Ephesians 6:12: "We are not fighting against flesh and blood enemies, but against evil rulers and authorities of the unseen world, against powers in this dark world, and against evil spirits in the heavenly places."

Identify the lies that are dragging you down and remove them. Then replace it with Truth. How can we access God's power to stop Satan's lies?

Roman 12: 2: "Do not conform to the pattern of this world, but be transformed by the renewing of your mind,"

Jesus said in John 8:32, "If you hold on to my teaching, you are really my disciples. Then you will know the truth, and the truth will set you free."

As you dive into truth, ask God to pinpoint the lie at the root of what is going on in your heart. No more trying to impress people or living a lie. It is time to walk in freedom; it's time to fight back and fill your mind with His Truth, the Holy inspired Word of God. It is time to change the way we think. God hasn't given us the spirit of fear but a spirit of power, love, and self-discipline. It's time for total surrender. It's time to lay it at His feet.

~58~

The Good Father

I was blessed with a great earthly father, and I will never forget what he taught me; he showed me how to live a life that counts. Watching him, I learned to work hard, invest in my family and put God first. I am blessed with so many great memories. I can see him still sitting on an old Coke crate, telling me, "Rare back and rock, give me your best fastball." He was ready for the next pitch if I hit the Mitt or bounced it at his feet. My Dad was always there! He never missed a practice and was always the first at all my games. He also ensured that our family was always in church and taught me right from wrong. His family was his passion; we were his heartbeat. He was our protector, and he watched over us like a hawk. I could go on and on about my earthly father, but I have to save room in this devotion to tell you about my Heavenly Father.

At five years of age, my earthly father led me to the throne of my Heavenly Father. I still remember the day I asked Jesus to take over my life. I remember the peace, love, and grace that overwhelmed me at a young age. Over the years, my Heavenly Father was always there in the good and bad times. He always places His family first, and He continues to provide for me every single day of my life.

I want to share Psalm 103:8-13 today; this scripture tells us some truth about my Heavenly Father. "The Lord is compassionate and gracious, slow to anger, abounding in love. He will not always accuse, nor will he harbor his anger forever; he does not treat us as our sins deserve or repay us according to our iniquities. For as high as the heavens are above the earth, so great is his love for those who fear him; as far as the east is from the west, so far he removed our transgression from us. As a father has compassion on his children, so the Lord has compassion on those who fear him."

Have you experienced the love of the Heavenly Father? Dive deep into His grace, compassion, and mercy today. Let Him carry your burdens, cover you with His goodness, and rest in His loving arms today. Then celebrate Him today. Worship Him today. He deserves all our praise and worship because He is the good Father.

~59~
The Word Became Flesh

John 1:14 says, "The Word became flesh and made his dwelling among us. We have seen his glory, the glory of the One and Only, who came from the Father, full of grace and truth."

God loved us so much that He sent His Son to be born in a lowly manger and become the world's Savior. So the beauty of the Christmas Truth is told in Luke 2:8-11:

"There were shepherds living out in the fields nearby, keeping watch over their flocks at night. An angel of the Lord appeared to them, and the glory of the Lord shone around them, and they were terrified. But the angel said to them, 'Do not be afraid, I will bring you good news of great joy that will be for all people. Today in the town of David, a Savior has been born to you; he is Christ the Lord.'"

That is good news—the good news of great joy for you and me. Before the Word came to earth, we were hopelessly lost in our sins. Man was desperately struggling to find peace and purpose.

Romans 3:23 says, "All have sinned and fall short of the glory of God."

Because of our sins, we deserve death and a place called Hell. Romans 6:23 tells us this truth:

113

"The wages of sin is death, but the gift of God is eternal life in Jesus Christ our Lord."

How could He send His only Son to this earth? Why did He allow His Son to come in human form to die on a rugged cross? Because God is full of grace and truth, and He desired fellowship with me and you. Jesus came to bring light to this dark and dying world.

John 14:6 Jesus said, "I am the way and the truth and the life. No one comes to the Father except through me."

We can't be good enough, we can't pay enough money, and we can't go to church enough to earn His love. But true life is only found through a relationship with Jesus.

John 1:9-12 gives us a promise to hang on to: "The true light that gives light to every man was coming into the world. He was in the world, and though the world was made through him, the world did not recognize him. He came to that which was his own, but his own did not receive him. Yet to all who received him, to those who believed in his name, he gave the right to become children of God."

Have you surrendered your heart and soul to the Savior of the world? Have you ever asked the Lord to forgive you, to wash your heart clean, and ask Him to take over? He is calling out today to bring light to the darkness.

~60~

What Goes In, Will Come Out

I grew up loving to play ball and loved going to the weight room with my buddies. We lifted weights, grunted a lot, and had a great time. I would be in great shape if I pushed all this weight around. What I didn't realize was that even more than what I do with my body, being fit is about what I put in my body. To be truly healthy, what I eat has to be healthy. I can't eat Krispy Kreme donuts daily and down a couple of Oreos before bed. The older I get, the harder it is to keep that belly fat off. I have to watch my sugar intake and make sure I watch my portions of food.

The same is true when it comes to our minds. What we put in our minds comes out in our lives. Romans 8:5-6 says this:

> *"Those who are dominated by the sinful nature think about sinful things, but those who are controlled by the Holy Spirit think about things that please the Spirit. So letting your sinful nature control your mind leads to death. But letting the Spirit control your mind leads to life and peace."*

Paul was teaching us this, if we allow thought in our mind, it will come out in our life. I am a straightforward person, and I wouldn't say I like to make things complicated. So, to change your life, you must change how you think. We need to be on guard about what we allow into our minds. We have to stop and ask ourselves some serious

115

questions. What are you constantly thinking about? What do you see on your phone, or what do you watch on TV? What kind of music do you play as you ride down the road? Who or what has your ear or your attention? Is what you are listening to negative or positive?

Are you taking in God's Word? Are you filling your mind with Truth constantly? Commit today to break the pattern of negative thoughts, worry, and expose the lies of Satan that he continually throws at you. Flood your minds with the things of God. Flood your heart with the Word of God. Expose the lies of the snake, and embrace the truth today. What are you allowing in your mind?

~61~
Take Time To Chew

In my early years growing up as a child, I remember my mom making me come in and eat. I would come to the dinner table, and my whole family would sit down and enjoy a meal together. But being a child who loved to play outside, I was in a hurry to get back outside to finish our game. So I rushed through the meal as fast as possible; I didn't take time to enjoy it or chew it that much. My mom always told me, "Dennis, slow down and make sure you chew your food, and wait thirty minutes before you start running again." In other words, take the time to digest your food.

As good Christian people, most of us get plenty of spiritual food. But, yes, we stay busy and always on the go. Many of our days are completely consumed, and there is no time to slow down and enjoy the day. We have to go to work because we have to pay the bills. We must take our kids and grandkids to all their activities and sports events. We must buy groceries, run errands, and make it to all the church services. Most of the time, we listen to the sermon on Sunday, and if we are feeling really good, we will check in at church on Wednesday. We take in God's Word, but do we take time to chew? Has your spiritual meal become something you have to do, or has it become something you are made to do? Do we digest all that God has placed on the table?

Look at Joshua 1:8 tells us, "Do not let this Book of the Law depart from your mouth; meditate on it day and night, so that you may be careful to do everything written in it."

I want to challenge you to take a daily dose of God's Word. Fill your plate up. Make it a priority in your life. Block out time in your busy day to feed on scripture. We all need our spiritual food to grow and mature as believers in Christ. We need our daily truth because it helps us recognize the devil's lies. But don't rush through your time with God; slow down, meditate, and digest what God is saying to you personally. Come to God's buffet table and eat all you want, but take time to chew and enjoy His goodness. May God bless you and your family today.

~62~

What Holds You On The Road

When life is full of sorrow and hard times, how do you deal with it? Do you hold it all in or do and act like nothing is wrong? Some of us can hide it so well until it finally gets to us, and then we explode, and our junk gets everywhere. Sometimes we try to stay busy, where we don't have to think about it, so we go and go until we become physically exhausted. We push off the reality of what is going on in our lives, and we push it to the side and hope everything will go away, and maybe we will walk away from this terrible dream. How do we handle bad news, those unexpected turns, and that crushing blow that knocks us to our knees? Life is so much more than gumballs, flowers, and party streamers. Life can get ugly fast, and one phone call can shatter all your hopes and dreams. In this life here on earth, bad news will find you sooner or later, and you will have to deal with heartache, depression, sorrow, and disappointment. So where do you run to when or what holds you on the road when life doesn't go as planned?

King David knew about the storms of life. He knew what it was like to struggle spiritually and deal with temptation. Yes, sometimes David failed miserably and fell right on his face. He dealt with some crazy family issues and unhealthy relationships. I guarantee you he was a victim of criticism, gossip, and lies. He was knocked down and chased, and people wanted him dead. Yet, how did he keep going with all this pressure, temptation, and heartache? How did he hold it in the road?

> Listen to David's prayer in Psalm 27:1-3, "The Lord is my light and my salvation-whom shall I fear? The Lord is my stronghold of my life-of whom shall I be afraid? When evil men advance against me to devour my flesh, when my enemies and my foes attack me, they will stumble and fall. Though an army besiege me, my heart will not fear; though war breaks out against me, even then will I be confident."

David's stronghold was his relationship with God. Over the years, David learned to turn to God and ask for help. He wasn't ashamed to cry out to God and ask for help.

Look at David's prayer in Psalm 86:1-8 which says this:

> "Hear, O Lord, and answer me, for I am poor and needy. Guard my life, for I am devoted to you. You are my God; save your servant who trusts in you. Have mercy on me, O Lord, for I call to you all day long. Bring joy to your servant, for to you, O Lord. I lift my soul. You are forgiving and good, O Lord, abounding in love to all who call to you. Hear my prayer, O Lord, listen to my cry for mercy. In the day of my trouble I will call to you, for you will answer me. Among the gods there is none like you, O Lord; no deeds can compare with yours."

Pray this prayer David prayed to the Lord, ask the Lord to guard your life, to show you mercy, and to bring you joy. He will help you hold it on the road during those difficult times.

~63~

Where's Your Praise?

Christmas celebration is over, all the presents are opened, and all left is the few small portions of leftover turkey. Now it is back to the same ole same ole. A few of you may have a few more days of vacation left, but many are returning to work to make a living. It's time to go back to the grind of life and face the same situations and problems that were there before the Christmas season hit. You are sitting there thinking, it was so much fun to give all those cool gifts to your children and grandchildren, but now you have to pay for them. The Christmas celebration gives you enough time to pause, helps you breathe joyfully, and takes your mind off the things that stress you out. For some reason, we all tend to focus on what is wrong in this world or what is wrong with our lives. Unfortunately, that kind of thinking will lead you down the wrong road.

> *Psalm 42:5 say: "Why, my soul, are you downcast? Why so disturbed within me? Put your hope in God, for I will yet praise him, my Savior and my God."*

Don't just look at what is wrong; take time to look at what is right. So I want to encourage you this morning by sharing Philippians 4:4-7 which says this:

> *"Rejoice in the Lord always. I will say it again: Rejoice! Let your gentleness be evident to all. The Lord is near. Do not be anxious about anything, but in*

every situation, by prayer and petition, with thanksgiving, present your request to God. And the peace of God, which transcends all understanding, will guard your hearts and minds in Christ Jesus."

Dig into that truth today to live this life with peace, joy, and happiness. Like you, I struggle with negative thoughts, worry about my children, and mostly live from paycheck to paycheck. But I know God's Word is true. Paul tells us that when life pulls you down and Satan attacks your mind with negative thoughts of hopelessness and despair, rejoice in the Lord. In the face of depression, grief, and negativity, rejoice in the Lord. He says to be anxious about nothing, but in every situation, walk into the presence of the Lord. Being in the presence of the Lord will change your perspective on life, and He will guard your heart and mind.

Romans 12:2 says, "Do not conform to the patterns of this world, but be transformed by the renewing of your mind, Then you will be able to test and approve what God's will is-his good and perfect will."

Take everything to your Heavenly Father today, and leave it all at His feet. Praise Him! There is nobody that loves you more; He cares for you. Approach the throne of grace with confidence, that we may receive mercy and find grace to help us in a time of need. When you see your mind turning towards the negative, recognize the attack, then turn up the praise. God bless you today.

~64~

Let The Light Break Through

I have a few days off to celebrate the New Year and complete a couple of projects at the house. The biggest task is to thin out the trees in my backyard. All the trees have grown together and will not allow sunlight to hit my lawn in my backyard. I have no grass but a good patch of clovers growing everywhere. So I took my trusty hatchet and began to take out a couple of big limbs. The sunlight started to shine through, so I continued to chop until my forearm was about to explode. About this time, I wished I had a chainsaw to finish the job; it would have been much more manageable. Hours of chopping finally paid off, and with all the limbs thinning out, I had a light covering my backyard in the hope of growing some pretty green grass. Now I had to pile everything up and drag everything to the road. Then the city will come and take it all away. I had to clean out the clutter of tree limbs to let the sunlight through, so my grass would have a chance to grow.

My question for you today is, what is cluttering your life? What is causing you not to get the proper Light so you can experience growth in your walk with Christ?

> *Colossians 3:5 says, "Put to death, therefore, whatever belongs to your earthly nature: sexual immorality, impurity, lust, evil desires and greed, which is idolatry."*

123

What is hindering your love relationship with your Heavenly Father? What has become more important to you than growing in the Lord? Has money become that limb you are allowing to grow in your life that consumes your thoughts?

> *Philippians 2:12-13 tells us, "Continue to work out your salvation with fear and trembling. For it is God who works in you to will and to act according to His good purpose."*

In other words, as believers in Christ, we must recognize what is hindering the Light from shining in our lives. Some work will be involved to get our "limbs to the road." God also has a responsibility, but you will never have to worry about Him doing His part. He will remove those hindrances when we drag them at His feet. He is faithful and just.

God is calling you to grow in Him. Growth requires light. What is blocking the Light in your walk with God? Identify it, do the work, and drag it to His feet. Then trust Him to do His part.

~65~
Security System?

Matthew 4:1-4 says, "Jesus was led by the Spirit into the wilderness to be tempted by the devil. After fasting for forty days and forty nights, he was hungry. The tempter came to him and said, "If you are the Son of God, tell these stones to become bread." Jesus answered, "It is written Man shall not live on bread alone, but on every word that comes from the mouth of God."

I don't have to tell you this, but Satan is a schemer who wants to destroy you. He will not attack you where you are strong but hit you where you are the weakest or not expecting it. The Word of God describes Satan as a liar, a thief, and one who will deceive you in a heartbeat. He will not come through your front door to rob you of joy, but he will look for an open side window, or he doesn't mind kicking in your back door at an unexpected time. So please don't put it past him to watch your home, life, and family.

My home was robbed a few years ago. My wife always took her lunch every day at the same time to let the dogs out and grabbed a quick bite before heading back to work. To her surprise, she found our home in a wreck. The back window was smashed, and glass was all over the floor. The back door was wide open, our bed was flipped over, and most of the things I held dear were gone. They came in broad daylight and robbed me of my valuables, security, and peace. The thief knew our routine, and they knew when and how to break in without getting caught. That week, I scheduled an appointment for a security system in my home. I wasn't going to stand by and let this happen again.

How has Satan robbed you? Is he watching your home, your life, and your family? You better believe it; the enemy plans to rob you of your joy, peace of mind, and passion for ministry. Are you prepared for when he hits you with temptation, covers you with lies, and sneaks in your back door? Set up your security system today, and hide God's Word in your heart. If it worked for Jesus, it would indeed work for you.

> Psalm 119:11 says, "I have hidden your word in my heart that I might not sin against you."

> Hebrews 4:12 tells us, "For the word of God is living and active. Sharper than any double-edged sword. It penetrates even to divide soul and spirit, joints and marrow; it judges the thoughts and attitudes of the heart."

Do not wait for Satan to hit, be prepared, and take in the Word of God to cover your home, life, and family.

~66~
Written In Red

Jesus is speaking in Luke chapter six, preaching one of his most famous sermons, the Beatitudes. I want to take you quickly to verse twenty-seven, and I want you to notice that it is written in red, which means these are the very words of Jesus. Jesus loved to teach and use parables; he wanted to get you to stop and think. But here in Luke 6:27-31, he was straightforward and wasn't mixing words. He said this:

> *"But I tell you who hear me: Love your enemies, do good to those who hate you, bless those who mistreat you. If someone strikes you on one check, turn to him the other also. If someone takes your cloak, do not stop him from taking your tunic. Give to everyone who asks you, and if anyone takes what belongs to you, do not demand it back. Do to others as you would have them do to you."*

That may be an easy read, but how hard is that to live out? Jesus didn't use fancy words or a creative story to get your attention. Instead, he was straightforward and laid it all on the table. How many have been done wrong, stolen from, or talked about unfairly? How many times have we been so full of pride that we demanded our rights or walked away from a situation because we were so mad?

Jesus was just getting started, then he continues in verses 35-36 and says:

127

"But love your enemies, do good to them, and lend to them without expecting to get anything back. Then your reward will be great, and you will be sons of the Most High, because he is kind to the ungrateful and wicked. Be merciful, just as your Father is merciful."

Wow, this is next-level Christianity, right? Not only am I called out of selfishness and pride, but we are to show mercy to our enemies. Jesus was not a preacher full of hot air; he lived out what he taught. His mercies are new every day, and He has shown me grace daily. His love is genuine, and his words are true. What situation has God brought to your attention today? What relationship has God pushed before your spiritual eyes that must be restored? Is there an issue of pride or unforgiveness that you must turn over to your Heavenly Father before you can go to someone to say you're sorry?

Ephesians 4:31-32 tell us, "Get rid of all bitterness, rage and anger, brawling and slander, along with every form of malice. Be kind and compassionate to one another, forgiving each other, just as in Christ God forgave you."

Get ready to walk out what God has shared with you today. Never forget God blesses obedience.

~67~
Three Charges To The Church

First Thessalonians 4:1-2 Paul writes, "Finally, brothers, we instructed you how to live in order to please God, as in fact you are living. Now we ask you and urge you in the Lord Jesus to do this more and more. For you know what instructions we gave you by the authority of the Lord Jesus."

Did you see Paul push, that gentle push? We were given a mission as believers in Jesus Christ. In Matthew 28:18-20 Jesus gave us our marching orders when he said:

"Go and make disciples of all nations, baptizing them in the name of the Father and of the Son and of the Holy Spirit, and teaching them to obey everything I have commanded you. And surely I am with you always, to the very end of the age."

Here is my question for all believers in Jesus: Are we on track with what God calls us to do and be? Is our focus on reaching the lost and then spending every bit of energy and money to disciple them in the ways of God? I am afraid most churches are more worried about maintaining their numbers and ensuring the existing crowd is happy and comfortable. Sometimes we are so inwardly focused that we lose sight of our purpose and commission. Most of us can quote the Great Commission, but are we walking it out daily?

I want to get straight to the point and make it simple. Paul gave three charges to the Church of Colosse and us today. Colossians 3:27-29 says this:

> *"To them God has chosen to make known among the Gentiles the glorious riches of this mystery, which is Christ in you, the hope of glory. We proclaim him, admonishing and teaching everyone with all wisdom, so that we may present everyone perfect in Christ. To this end I labor, struggling with all his energy, which so powerfully works in me."*

There are three things Paul said to do as a church, and do them all with passion. First, proclaim the Lord Jesus. Secondly, teach the Holy Scriptures. Last but not least, reach the world for Jesus Christ. We are to seek to present every man complete or mature in Christ. In other words, make the name of Jesus famous worldwide. We can't continue to do what we have always done without reaching people for Christ.

Let's make it personal. How many people have you personally shared with this past year about the difference Christ has made in your life? How many people have you walked to the foot of the cross in 2023? I am not trying to be ugly or tick anybody off, but we all tend to get off track and get lost in things that are good but not what is best. Peter Lord probably said it best, "The main thing is to keep the main thing the main thing. Proclaim the Lord Jesus. Teach the Holy Scriptures and reach the world for the glory of God. Go and tell.

~68~

A Good "Go By"

I worked for AT&T for a long time. Most of my time there was spent as a manager, designing fiber runs and other fiber services. I met many incredible people and am very grateful for my time there. One thing is sure when it comes to technology, the design to make everything work constantly changes. At times, that made my job difficult. No job was ever the same, but it did help to have what I called a 'Go By.' A 'Go By' was a job approved, met all the standards, and has already worked in the field. That job was proven to work, giving me direction to design a good design, especially if it was a designer with a good reputation.

Today, I want to give you a good 'Go By' we can follow when praying for others. Paul was a mighty man of God, and he was a man of action. Not only did he talk a good game, but he also walked it out; he was a prayer warrior. Look at Paul's prayer that he prays for the saints at Ephesus, and sense the genuineness of his prayer for knowledge and power for the Church.

> Paul prays in Ephesians 1:16-19, "I have not stopped giving thanks for you, remembering you in my prayers. I keep asking that the God of our Lord Jesus Christ, the glorious Father, may give you the Spirit of wisdom and revelation, so that you may know him better. I pray also that the eyes of your heart may be enlightened in order that you may know the hope to

which he has called you, the riches of his glorious inheritance in the saints and his incomparably great power for us who believe."

Paul prayed that the Church would receive the Spirit of wisdom and revelation to know God better. Then he prayed that the eyes of their hearts be enlightened, that they may know their hope in Jesus. Now that is a good 'Go By.'

I dare you to pray this scripture over your leaders at church. I double-dog dare you to pray it over your family and friends. I also want to challenge you to pray this prayer over your own life and be ready to be amazed by God. He wants to show us so many things, but we must be prepared to receive them. This is a great "Go By."

-69-

Wise Word From Paul

I love getting up in the morning, grabbing coffee, and spending time alone with God. It's a time of refreshing and a time of getting focused for my day. Some mornings, it's time to unload all my cares and worries of this hectic life. It's a time of praise, petition, and digging into God's Word. I may read a couple of verses, or I may read twenty chapters. This morning God opened a window of truth in Paul's writings in the book of Romans. It wasn't anything that grabbed me and shook me, but it was so practical and straightforward. Words of wisdom will help us as believers in Jesus Christ.

> *Romans 12:9-16 says this, "Love must be sincere. Hate what is evil; cling to what is good. Be devoted to one another in brotherly love. Honor one another above yourself. Never be lacking in zeal, but keep your spiritual fervor, serving the Lord. Be joyful in hope, patient in affliction, faithful in prayer. Share with God's people who are in need. Practice hospitality. Bless those who persecute you; bless and do not curse. Rejoice with those who rejoice; mourn with those who mourn. Live in harmony with one another. Do not be proud, but be willing to associate with people of low position. Do not be conceited."*

We can read right over these verses and move on with our life. We can make ourselves feel good knowing that we read the Bible today, or we can make it personal and apply the medication that God is prescribing. For example:

What pet sin do you keep hanging on to, and Satan wears you out repeatedly? What evil do you need to hate? What good do you need to cling on to? I encourage you to talk it out with your Heavenly Father today. Look at all your relationships; whom do you need to honor? Have you been selfish with your time and have yet to show someone close to you how much you love them? What can you do to show them honor today? Do you see where I am going? Are you patient in affliction? We all could sit down and whine to God all day long over this one. Unfortunately, pain seems to hunt us down and stalks us daily, and we can do nothing about it in most cases.

I encourage you to read through this scripture again and make it personal. Allow yourself some time to hear the voice of God about the practical things of your life. What changes must we make to become better dads or moms? Lord, bless my friends today and let them see your Word in a new light. Wrap them up in your love, comfort them, and let your light shine brightly in their lives.

~70~
The Big But

One of the greatest joys in my calling is writing a devotional every day. I love taking in the Word of God, but God has shown me that I also need to give it away over the years. Expressing the Word through writing creates a continuous flow of the Spirit in my life. I know the difference God's Word has made in my life, and I want the world to experience it for themselves. My calling is to encourage those around me, wherever I may be. I want people to know that God loves you no matter where you are in life. No matter what sins you have committed or how many times you have failed Him, He still adores and welcomes you with open arms. He is not a God out to get revenge or destroy you, but he wants to share His incredible love and wrap you up in His arms.

> Ephesians 2:1-3 says this, "As for you, you were dead in your transgressions and sins, in which you used to live when followed the way of this world and of the ruler of the kingdom of the air, the spirit who is now at work in those who are disobedient. All of us lived among them at one time, gratifying the cravings or our sinful nature and following its desires and thoughts. Like the rest, we were by nature objects of wrath."

Paul is talking about our life before Christ; does it sound familiar? Now I want to talk about the big but found in verse four. Yes, at one time, we were lost, hopeless, and depressed because we had no hope. But thank God for this in the following scriptures. Here is the good news that is found in Ephesians 2:4-9:

> "But because of his great love for us, God, who is rich in mercy, made us alive with Christ even when we were dead in transgressions-it is by grace you have been saved. And God raised us up with Christ and seated us with him in the heavenly realms in Christ Jesus, in order that in the coming ages he might show the incomparable riches of his grace, expressed in his kindness to us in Christ Jesus. For it is by grace you have been saved, through faith-and this not from yourselves, it is the gift of God-not by works, so that no one can boast."

There is life found in a relationship with Jesus Christ. We, the Church, must share this Good News and shout it from the rooftops. "Thank you, Lord, for the grace and mercy you show us daily." We deserved death, BUT God showed us grace.

~71~
Whom Are You Imitating?

As a child, I remember waking up and finding my dad shaving his face in the bathroom. We only had one bathroom; there wasn't another bathroom to go to. Putting white foamy stuff on your face was the coolest thing to rack off with a razor. I always wanted to be like my dad, so I watched how he shaved every morning. I studied each stroke to see how it was done. As time went by, I felt like I was ready to shave at the ripe age of five. Of course, my dad said, "You have a while before you need to shave; give it some time." I was persistent and never gave up asking to shave to be just like him. One morning, to my surprise, he gave me a razor of my own. I didn't know then, but he gave me his old razor with no blade. I thought it was Christmas that morning; I stood beside my dad and shaved just like him. I followed his every move and imitated every stroke of his razor.

The older I got, I found other people to imitate too. I loved playing sports as a child and fell in love with pitching. During Middle School, Orel Hershiser was among the most dominant pitchers in the Major Leagues. He played for the Los Angeles Dodgers and was my favorite pitcher then. I took time to read every article I could find, remembering that we didn't have the internet then. Sports Illustrated produced a report one year highlighting one of his most incredible seasons. I studied the pictures, checked out his technique, learned how he held the ball and knew what kind of glove he wore on the field. I did my best to imitate him in every way.

Here is the question I want to ask you today, whom are you imitating? Paul wrote these words in Ephesians 5:1-2 and said,

> *"Be imitators of God, therefore, as dearly and live a life of love, just as Christ loved us and gave himself up for us as a fragrant offering and sacrifice to God."*

That is a tall task; it is easier to say than live out. But just like I did with my dad and Orel Hershiser, I study Jesus' every move, watch how he treated people, and imitate His every move here on earth.

> *John 3:30 says, "He must become greater; I must become less."*

~72~
Woe To The Man

I remember Bellsouth issuing me a bag phone to use in my company car many years ago; I thought I was high class. It was so cool to talk in your car; man, did I feel special? But look how far cell phones have come today; the technology and what it can do will blow you away. It's like a personal computer that you can carry everywhere. Yes, in some cases, it has made our life much easier and more productive, but Satan also uses it to attack your minds and eat up valuable time with friends and family. Let me tell you; it's an easy trap to get sucked into. How much time a day do you spend with your phone in your hand? Can you go through a meal without looking at your phone? How many times a day do you check your likes from the post you put up that morning? It can become an addiction.

Look at what Jesus said in Matthew 18:7-9, "Woe to the world because of the things that cause people to sin! Such things must come, but woe to the man through whom they come! If your hand or your foot causes you to sin, cut it off and throw it away. It is better for you to enter life maimed or crippled than to have two hands or two feet and be thrown into the eternal fire. And if your eye causes you to sin, gouge it out and throw it away. It is better for you to enter life with one eye than to have two eyes and be thrown in the fire of hell."

I am not telling you to gouge your eye out or throw your cell phone in the trash, but I encourage you to guard your mind and time. Satan will do anything to take you down and cause you to be more dependent on your phone than God.

The challenge for today: Limit how many times you look at your cell phone today. Please notice how many times you pick it up and look at it. Be on your guard against popups and things that will cause you to lust. Stand firm in your faith today.

~73~
ESPN

I have one hundred and ninety channels I can watch on TV. Out of those one hundred and ninety channels, ESPN stands alone at the top as my favorite channel to watch. I love to watch sports, but I don't have time to waste sitting down and watching all the games. Instead, I can watch a thirty-minute segment of ESPN and be caught up on all the games. So I know who won the game, what coaches called the wrong play, and who made the play of the game. ESPN offers all the highlights, best players, and plays. That is why I pay all that money for satellite TV. I want to see the amazing catches, the tough run where they broke three tackles, then ran somebody over. I want to see all the fantastic dunks, where they soar from the free-throw line and throw down a hard slam. I love seeing a 450' home run in a crucial part of a playoff game. Those are just some of the great sports highlights, just a little taste of the greatness of the athletes. But most of the time, ESPN doesn't show you the road that most great athletes take to achieve excellence.

They don't show you all the days they get up before sunrise when nobody is screaming their names. They don't offer all the sacrifices each great athlete has to make daily to compete at a very high level. We don't see all the injuries, the mental struggle, the fatigue, and all the frustration each great athlete goes through. To become great at something, there has to be a process of sacrifice, discipline, and a willingness to put in the blood, sweat, and tears. Of course, we all would love to be a part of the highlight reel, but are we willing to put in the blood, sweat, and tears? Achieve greatness as an athlete in a process; it will not happen overnight. Yes, it is a God-given talent, but they must work.

> Romans 6:12 says, "Therefore, do not let sin reign in your mortal body so that you obey its evil desires."

Does God make way for us to live a holy life here on earth? He sure does, He gives us everything we need to overcome Satan's schemes and traps, but He has given us a responsibility to live a holy life. The first thing we should notice in this scripture is that the pursuit of holiness is not allowing sin to reign in our mortal body- it is something we must commit to. Paul's statement here is one of exhortation. He addressed himself to our wills. He said, "Do not let sin reign," implying that this is something for which we are responsible. The experience of holiness is not a gift we receive but something we are called to work at. As believers, we all have received the gift of salvation through the blood of Christ. Yes, we can celebrate this, and we need to tell the world about His amazing grace. But now it's time to put in the work; it is time to face the grind of life and live out our lives in a way that pleases the Father. We love to see the highlights of great men and women of God, but you never get to see all the bumps, bruises, and sacrifices they make along the way. So keep your head up, keep pressing forward, and know that God is working through all the stuff you face today. It's great to dream, but daily work accompanies that dream.

~74~
Perfect Love

What are your regrets? What are your fears? What are your weaknesses? How can you grow? How can you overcome those insecurities?

> *First John 4:16-18 tells us this, "God is love. Whoever lives in love lives in God, and God in him. In this way, love is made complete among us so that we will have confidence on the day of judgment, because in this world we are like him. There is no fear in love, But perfect love drives out fear, because fear has to do with punishment. The one who fears is not made in perfect love."*

Perfect love drives out fear. If we were honest with ourselves, some things would have been with us for a long time! What have you always wanted to do, but fear has always held you back? Fear is a liar, and it will keep you captive. Getting caught up in the mundane way of life is so easy. Don't let life be about going to work, paying bills, sleeping, and waking up the following day to do it all over again. So, I want to challenge you today to commit to lifelong learning. Don't be scared to try something new and dare to dream. But when you dream, dream big because we serve a huge and mighty God.

I will be upfront and honest with you; learning something new isn't always going to feel warm and fuzzy. There will be times when you stumble and fall. There will also be times of incredible frustration. Just know that it is all a part of the process. It's God's way of teaching us how to think, pray things through, and place our total trust in Him. A continual learner learns how to deal with setbacks and develops a sense of creativity. I encourage you to take your eyes off your regrets and fears and place them on God's love for you.

The challenge for Today: Stop looking in the rear-view mirror, take your eyes off the past, and push fears away that have knocked you to your feet. Keep your eyes centered on Jesus Christ, rest in His perfect love, and listen to what He says about you. Take time to see what God is doing around you, then jump in and serve with passion.

-75-

Waiting In The Silence

The noise of this world gets louder and louder. When was the last time you got away by yourself, away from your radio, television, and your cell phone? When did you previously wait in silence with no music playing, no Facebook to respond to, and no internet access? And we wonder why we don't hear from God. I am so guilty of always having to have noise around me; I even fall asleep with the television playing. It drives me crazy to sit in a room where nobody is talking, so I try my best to start a conversation. Is that weird, or what? While confessing my faults, I might as well own up to another thing that drives me crazy, waiting drives me crazy. The older I get, the harder it is to wait. I become irritated when I have to wait in traffic or in a long line to get food. My wife gives me a hard time when we go out to eat on Friday nights because I try my best to leave the house before the clock strikes five; we have to beat the dinner rush; it's a matter of life or death. Then God gives me a devotion title with the two things I struggle with. Do you think He is trying to tell me something?

I want to give you some verses the Lord dropped on me today. Lamentations 3:22-28 says:

"Because of the Lord's great love we are not consumed, for his compassion never fail. They are new every morning; great is your faithfulness. I say to myself, 'The Lord is my portion; therefore I will wait for

him.' The Lord is good to those whose hope is in him, to the one who seeks him; it is good to wait quietly for the salvation of the Lord. It is good for a man to bear the yoke while he is young. Let him sit alone in silence, for the Lord has laid it on him."

Psalm 37:7 says, "Be still before the Lord and wait patiently for him; do not fret when men succeed in their ways, when they carry out their wicked schemes."

Psalm 46:10 says, "Be still and know that I am God; I will be exalted among the nations, I will be exalted in the earth."

Have you ever been grateful for words you didn't want to hear? "Lord, prick our hearts today. Lord, speak loud and clear to the issues of our hearts. Please help us be still, pull away from the noise of this world, and turn our attention to your face. Lord, thank you for your patience with us in my weaknesses; I know we sometimes act like spoiled children, but help us to be able to wait on You in the silence. "Thank you for the goodness you show us new every day. Expose the distractions in our lives, and hit us with Your high beams."

~76~
Constant Flow

The Sea of Galilee is a freshwater lake in Israel approximately 33 miles in circumference. It is about 13 miles long and about 8.1 miles wide. The maximum depth is 141 feet deep. It is also 186 feet below sea level. The lake is fed partly by an underground spring, although its primary source is the Jordan River, which flows north and south. Notice I said it flows through it. The Sea of Galilee has an inlet and an outlet. This well-known Biblical Sea is where a South Georgia boy would love to go with a rod and a purple worm! It is beautiful, crystal-clear water, and the plant life is unbelievable.

But there is another body of water in Israel that is the opposite. Of course, I am talking about the Dead Sea. Like the Sea of Galilee, it is fed by the Jordan River, but the Dead Sea doesn't have an outlet. That is why the Dead Sea has a vast concentration of salt and other mineral deposits. And it is hard for vegetation and fish life to live there. To be healthy and grow in wisdom, we need a constant flow of Christ in our lives! Yes, we need to receive from the Lord; we require that steady, continuous flow of God's goodness and wisdom. That comes by digging into God's Word. We receive by sitting under godly teachings and taking in truth. Yes, we accept it in our time of worship and meditation. But just like the Sea of Galilee, we need an outlet. We are not called just to gather and take in good information and wisdom. But we are called to give it away.

We are called to go and make disciples! Matthew 28:18-20 Jesus said:

> *"All authority in heaven and on earth has been given to me, Therefore go and make disciples of all the nations, baptizing them in the name of the Father and of the Son and of the Holy Spirit, and teaching them to obey everything I have commanded you, And surely I am with you always, to the very end of the age."*

That was Jesus' last words to us as a Church before He ascended to heaven. That is known as the Great Commission, not the Great Suggestion. It's not an option but a command from our Heavenly Father. We will become healthy and grow in wisdom as we receive from the Lord and give it to others. As believers, we need God's constant steady flow in our lives.

-77-

911

We live in a day like no other, a world where there is so much confusion, depression, hopelessness, and strife. Every country is covered in fear and chaos, and the tension grows daily. We live in a time when most people's outlook on life is negative and critical of others. It's a time when we all smile less and complain more. It's easy to fall into the pit of discouragement and become overwhelmed, but I want to encourage you today to rise above it all and praise our glorious King. Praise His name when you struggle to pay your bills and seem like you will never get out of debt. When family issues never disappear, and you want everybody to get along, praise His name. Praise His name when you have been sick for three weeks and are not improving.

What would you do if someone tried to break into your house? Would you sit back, watch a little television, and eventually open the front door and ask them to come in? That would be ridiculous. I hope your first call is 911, then take every step necessary to scare away the thief. If you have an alarm system, trip it and let the alarm go off. Make sure everybody knows what is going on. My question is, why do we allow depression to snoop around our house? Why let fear hang out at night at our back door? We can't just sit there and open the door to our house and allow them to walk in and rob us of joy. That would be crazy. Fight back!

David wrote a powerful message to us in Psalm 145:1-5 which said this:

> "I will exalt you, my God, the King; I will praise your name forever and ever. Every day I will praise you and extol your name for ever and ever. Great is the Lord and most worthy of praise; his greatness no one can fathom. One generation will commend your works to another; they will tell of your mighty acts. They will speak of the glorious splendor of your majesty, and I will meditate on your wonderful works."

When the thief of this world comes to attack your home, don't just sit there and feel sorry for yourself; turn up the volume of praise, and protect your house. The thief hates to hear the glory that belongs to the REAL King. He is so selfish, self-centered, and full of himself; praise going up to our Heavenly Father will cause him to flee. So sound the alarm, load your soul with praise, then blast it as loud as possible. Guard your house with praise.

~78~
Circle Your Answer

If I ask you today, what motivates you to get out of bed daily? How would you respond? What or who are you living for? For many Georgia fans, it was to win one more National Championship. Yes, I was excited to see Georgia win, it was a great game to watch, and we had a great time with family. I still can't believe I stayed up to watch the entire game; that was way past my bedtime. What is your purpose in this life? What drives you? What are your goals and your dreams? The last question I want to ask you before we get into scripture is whether your answers to these questions align with God's purpose for your life.

Paul is writing in Second Corinthians 5:13-15 and says:

> *"If we are out of our mind, it is for the sake of God; if we are in our right mind, it is for you. For Christ's love compels us, because we are convinced that one died for all, and therefore all died. And he died for all, that those who live should no longer live for themselves but for him who died for them and was raised again."*

Wow, let the Word of God open your spiritual eyes this morning. Take the time to see and appreciate what the Father has done for us. He showed us grace; He gave His only Son to suffer and die on a rugged cross. Through the blood of Jesus, the Father opened the doors of Heaven so we could have access to the fellowship of our Lord. Let me say it this way, Jesus died for us, He gave us His all, and He held nothing back. This expression of God's love is our motivation for living! Because He lives, we can face tomorrow, and all fear is gone. Paul is saying to us today, those who are alive in your spirit because you have received Jesus, we should no longer live for ourselves, but for Him who died for us. Paul continues to write and says in 2 Corinthians 5:17:

> *"Therefore, if you are in Christ, he is a new creation; the old has gone, the new has come."*

The old way of living is over! He has something much better just around the corner; embrace His passion and purposes for your life. Don't get sidetracked by earthly wealth, selfish ambitions, and empty desires. Instead, invest in those things that will put a smile on the Father's face. Don't just breeze over this devotional, but I challenge you to take the time to answer these questions and try your best to be honest with yourself. Who are you living for? Christ or self? Circle your answer.

~79~
Build On A Good Foundation

We all have those times when we must tear down the walls we have allowed to exist. We all fall short, and we mess up along the way. But having a God who understands and shows us so much grace is good. "Thank you, Lord, for the gift of forgiveness and mercy. Thank you for lifting me and encouraging me daily! Thank you, God, for the privilege to come before you when I need to say sorry; forgive me. Thank you for tearing down that old wall of sin in my heart." Yes, be thankful, but this is just the beginning of what God has for us as children of God. Not only does God want to break down the old walls of our lives, but He wants us to build a solid foundation. A foundation that is solid and will stand firm even when the worst storms come our way.

> *Matthew 7: 24-25 Jesus tells us, "Therefore everyone who hears these words of mine and puts them into practice is like a wise man who built his house on the rock. The rain came down, the streams rose, and the winds blew and beat against that house; yet it did not fall, because it had its foundation on the rock."*

What is your life built on? Before I go any further, I want to ensure you have a personal walk with Jesus Christ. Has there been a time in your life when you have come face to face with Jesus? Have you had an encounter with the Living God of the universe? Being a Christian and a Christ follower isn't about our church attendance. It is not about doing good deeds or being morally good. It's about a personal relationship with Jesus and making Him the foundation that everything is built. It knows that the eternal God made a way for us to come to Him. Knowing and believing that He gave us His one and only Son to die on an old rugged cross, but also thinking Jesus didn't stay in that grave! This foundation is alive and well today, knowing that Jesus overcame sin and death. "Thank you, Lord!"

> *Revelations 3:20 says, "Here I am! Behold I stand at the door and knock. If anyone hears my voice and opens the door, I will come in and eat with him, and he with me."*

Have you answered that knock? Have you given your life to Jesus? Have you told Him thank you for what He has done for you? Have you ever asked him to come in and take over? Here is where it all begins.

Every builder needs to have a solid foundation. It needs to meet certain specifications. It has to be able to handle the weight of the load. That foundation in a believer's life is a personal relationship with Jesus Christ. When the storms come and the water rises, will your foundation be able to stand? Money, power, position, and popularity will crumble under the weight of the load! Build on something that will last and stand the test of time. When we come to the end of ourselves and receive Jesus as our Lord and Savior, He becomes that foundation forever and ever. Yes, there will be tough times in life, and there will be struggles along the way. But we have a promise in Christ that is found in Hebrews 13:5. It reads like this:

"Keep your lives free from the love of money and be content with what you have, because God has said, "Never will I leave you; never will I forsake you."

That is a promise from God Himself! He is my protector and my Heavenly Father. The great I AM—the God of heaven and earth. The all-knowing and all-powerful God of the universe, and I call Him Father because of what Jesus has done for me.

~80~

Waiting

Waiting for something that you want takes work. What about that prayer request that has been on your heart for years? Have you ever prayed for that wayward child, that they would give up that crazy living and begin to follow the Lord? You keep hoping, you keep praying, and you wait. Have you ever felt like the more intense you pray, the further you seem to wander away from the Lord? You have done everything you know to get them to the throne of God; you have read all books, threatened them, and shown them grace. Then you wait. Have you ever arrived at a place where your faith begins to run low? We both believe it will come to pass when God promises us something. But it will be in His timing and not ours. Part of our growth as believers in Christ involves waiting on God and standing on His promises.

What about Joseph? In Genesis chapter 37, God told Joseph in a dream,

> *"You are going to be a great leader, you will rule over all your brothers and the entire nation."*

After he shared that with his brothers, they threw him in a pit and sold him into slavery. Joseph caught a few breaks, and things began to look up. He found favor with Potiphar in chapter 39, but then his wife falsely accused him and sent him to prison. Have you ever been through the ups and downs of this life? It's like riding a rollercoaster, there are some super highs, and then the bottom will drop out from under you. Joseph was stuck in that prison for something he didn't do; years later, God delivered Joseph from prison, finally fulfilled His promise to Joseph, and elevated him to second in command over all of Egypt. Joseph had to wait.

We all, sooner or later, will have to wait. My question to you this morning is this: What do you do while you wait? What do you do while you wait for the promise of God? You have been dreaming about starting a new ministry and are so excited; you know that God has placed this in your heart. But that door isn't popping up; it seems like it is jammed, and there is no way that door will ever open. Maybe you are single and have been praying for the right man or woman to drop right before you, but time passes, and your faith tank is running low. So, you wait. Here is my second question: What does a waiter do? They wait on customers, and they serve them. When we are waiting, we should be serving God the entire time. In that waiting time of life, serve God with all your heart. While we are waiting on God's promise, serve Him with everything you have. When your life seems on hold, serve God because there is plenty to do. Have you ever noticed how much faster time passes when you do something constructive?

> *Colossians 3:17: "Whatever you do, whether in word or deed, do it all in the name of the Lord Jesus." While you wait, serve God with all your heart. He is faithful."*

~81~

We Want Answers

I will be the first to say I don't have all the answers to life's difficult questions. But, if I were honest with you, I have questions along the way that I need to ask. Sometimes, we all struggle with doubt, questions, and a lack of faith. But honest questions, doubts, and the hurts of this life can draw us closer to God than we ever dreamed.

Has the 'Why's' ever got you down or overwhelmed you in the thick of life? Why did it have to end in divorce? Why did God take him at such an early age? Why did I also struggle with money? Why did I get cancer, and why did I lose my job? These are some legitimate questions that we all ask, and we begin to wonder, is God even listening? Throughout the Bible, people struggled over God's involvement in their lives; trust me, you're not alone.

Mark 9:17-22 says, "A man in the crowd answered, 'Teacher. I brought you my son, who is possessed by a spirit that has robbed him of speech. Whenever it seizes him, it throws him to the ground. He foams at the mouth, gnashes his teeth and becomes rigid. I asked your disciples to drive out the spirit, but they could not.' 'O unbelieving generation,' Jesus replied, 'how long shall I stay with you? How long shall I put up with you? Bring the boy to me.' So they brought him. When the spirit saw Jesus, it immediately threw the boy into a convulsion. He fell to the ground and rolled around, foaming at the mouth. Jesus asked the boy's father, 'How long has he been like this?' 'From childhood,' he answered. It has often thrown him into fire or water to kill him. But if you can do anything, take pity on us and help us.'"

This father had serious doubts about Jesus healing his son, and I am sure he has been asked why for years. Look how Jesus responded to the boy's father in Mark 9:23:

"If you can?' said Jesus. 'Everything is possible for him who believes.'"

Can you imagine the pain this father has been carrying for years? When our children are hurting, we, as parents, are hurting too. But this close encounter with Jesus was about to change his life forever.

Mark 9:24 says this, "Immediately the boy's father exclaimed, 'I do believe; help me overcome my unbelief!'"

We all need to confess our unbelief and doubts but also turn to Jesus and trust Him with our most precious gifts. I challenge you to pray to the Father today: Lord, restore my hope in you. "Lord, free me from doubt and depression and help me in my unbelief. Please help me to overcome my unbelief and give me the guts to trust you in every situation that life throws at me. I believe you are the Son of God, and I know you hold the world in your hand. Draw me close to you today, wrap me up in your loving arms, and surround me with your comfort. Amen."

~82~

Ask Away

Matthew 7:7-8 says, "Ask and it will be given to you; seek and you will find; knock and the door will be open to you. For everyone who asks receives; the one who seeks finds; and though the one who knocks, the door will be opened."

The longer we live, the more questions we seem to have. So if you have questions, ask away. Just be prepared when God answers. Have you ever noticed how God the Son handled the situation when the Pharisees asked Him difficult questions while He was on earth? Jesus answered them with a question in return. He wasn't putting them off but getting them to think.

I questioned God when my two buddies died in their forties. Robert was a man after God's own heart; he was one of the godliest men I ever knew. He just left a great-paying job to serve the Lord as a full-time pastor at a local church. Robert gave his all to that church and that community; no one in that county didn't love Robert. Then he died unexpectedly of heart issues. He left way too early! It didn't make sense. I also lost a friend named Gregg, who struggled with diabetes; he was the group's jokester and kept you laughing in every situation. He was unique. When God made Gregg, he broke the mold. He was a great friend, but he, too, left this world way too early. These two guys made a difference in the community, and they loved everybody they knew. Lord, I don't understand; it didn't make sense. Why not take the thug on the street, breaking into houses and stealing everyone blind? When I saw them go so young and leave many family and friends behind hurt, I questioned God, and I did ask Him why.

The prophet Habakkuk knew firsthand what we were talking about. He slipped into the valley and experienced a crisis of belief. He struggled with how God seemed to be sitting on His hands and doing nothing about Babylon coming into Judah and taking over. How could this be?

> Habakkuk 1:12-13 says this, "Lord, are you not from everlasting? My God, my Holy One, you will never die. You, Lord, have appointed them to them to execute judgment; you, my Rock, have ordained them to punish. Your eyes are too pure to look at evil; you cannot tolerate wrongdoing. Why then do you tolerate the treacherous? Why are you silent while the wicked swallow up those more righteous than themselves?"

He is asking God, "Why don't you do something?" We have to remember that God sees the big picture. We need to come to that point in life when we learn to trust Him even when we can't feel him and believe in Him when it doesn't make sense. I don't know about you, but I have learned much more in the Valley of Life than on the mountaintops. It's ok to ask God questions; just be prepared when He answers you. Life will be full of valleys and mountaintop experiences; learn to enjoy them.

Dennis L Taylor

-83-
We Need Each Other

Ecclesiastes 4:9-12 says, "Two are better than one, because they have a good return for their work: If one falls down, his friend can help him up. But pity the man who falls and has someone to help him up! Also, if two lie down together, they will keep warm. But how can one keep warm alone? Though one may be overpowered, two can defend themselves. A cord of three strands is not quickly broken."

Hellen Keller said, "Walking with a friend in the dark is better than walking alone in the light. I don't care how strong or intelligent you are; we all need encouragement along the way. Our friendships are so meaningful and one of the best investments we could ever make. You see, God didn't design us to do life alone.

Have you ever sat down and taken the time to thank God for all of your friends? Have you ever noticed how different some of them are from each other? I believe God blesses us with all different kinds of friends so that they can help us in various ways. Do you have that friend who encourages you to dream big? We all need someone who will give us a vision of who we can be, far beyond anything we ever imagined. I need people who stretch my vision and challenge me to pray dangerous prayers. There was a time when all I wanted to do was to retire and take it easy, but thank God there were friends around me that pushed me to

162

listen to the Father's voice and dared to dream. Do you have friends around you that sharpen you?

> Proverbs 27:17 says, "As iron sharpens iron, so one man sharpens another."

Make sure you have those friends around you that make you better, someone who will hold you accountable for how you live your life. We need friends to pray for us, challenge us, and show us how to live godly.

> First Samuel 18:1 says, "After David had finished talking with Saul, Jonathan became one in spirit with David, and he loved him as himself."

Do you have a Jonathan in your life? That friend who truly cares about you comforts you when things are falling apart and is always there to listen. Last but not least, we all need that friend to kick our backside and do it in love. Tail kickers are those who love us enough to tell us the truth. We won't always like what they say, but sometimes it's what we need to move forward. They are the ones that challenge us not to settle, and they always remind us to get back up when we fall.

True friends are true wealth. So count your blessings today, and name them one by one. Take time today to lift a prayer of thanksgiving for those friends in your life, and make sure to pray for each one. I hope you have an awesome day.

~84~

Persecuted?

Hebrews 11:32-40 says this, "And what more shall I say? I do not have time to tell about Gideon, Barak, Sampson, Jephthah, David, Samuel, and the prophets, who through faith conquered kingdoms, administered justice, and gained what was promised; who shut the mouth of lions, quenched the fury of the flames, and escaped the edge of the sword; whose weakness was turned to strength; and who became powerful in battle and routed foreign armies. Women received back their dead, raised to life again. Others were tortured and refused to be released, so that they might gain a better resurrection. Some faced jeers and flogging, while still others were chained and put in prison. They were stoned; they were sawed in two; they were put to death by the sword. They went about in sheepskins and goatskins, destitute, persecuted and mistreated-the world was not worthy of them. They wandered in deserts and mountains, and in caves and holes in the ground. These were all commended for their faith, yet none of them received what had been promised. God had planned something better for us so that only together with us would they be made perfect."

Reading this, I had to stop and ask myself a crazy question, "What would the men and women in the early church think about the American Church today?" Don't get me wrong, Christians today face persecution, and I believe it will worsen as time passes. But I know some believers who don't want to go to church when it rains because it would mess up their hair. Or those chairs don't sit well; it hurts my back. We all can come up with so many excuses because we don't live a life that is completely sold out to Jesus Christ.

Jesus began to teach one of the most famous sermons ever preached. Matthew 5:1-2 says this:

> *"Now when he saw the crowds, he went up on a mountainside and sat down. His disciples came to him, and he began to teach them."*

Jesus began to share with them the eighth beatitude. In verses 3-9, Jesus rolled off seven beatitudes, all one sentence a piece. But in Matthew 5:10-12 Jesus shared the eighth beatitude, which said this:

> *"Blessed are those who are persecuted because of righteousness, for theirs is the kingdom of heaven. Blessed are you when people insult you, persecute you and falsely say all kinds of evil against you because of me. Rejoice and be glad, because great is your reward in heaven, for in the same way they persecuted the prophets who were before you."*

Church, it is time to count the cost and be willing to go all in with Christ. We can't back down or waiver in our faith. We live in a time when the Church has to stand up for what we believe and get out of our comfort zones. This world needs to know about the saving grace of Jesus Christ, and they need to know how much He loves them, no matter what.

Ask the Lord today to give you strength and courage as you live out your faith. First, empty yourself of selfishness and pride, then ask Him to fill you with the Holy Spirit to the point of overflowing. Then, when those hard times come, keep pressing forward, never back down, and don't give up. He is for you, who can stand against you. So let's stand Church and take the land for the glory of God.

~85~

What Are You Full Of?

Romans 15:13 says, "May the God of hope fill you with all joy and peace as you trust in him, so that you may overflow with hope by the power of the Holy Spirit."

What are you full of today? That may be a tricky question today, but how would your closest friends answer that question? Have you ever wondered why some people are more effective than other people? Why do some people enjoy life while others endure it? Why do some people take off and soar, and other people sink? I know that is a lot of questions, but I wanted to get you thinking today.

Thriving people thrive for a reason. They are committed to things that produce strength and hope. As a pastor, I have to stop occasionally and ask myself, What is the most important thing I need as a leader? My answer; I have to stay encouraged. If I am not encouraged, I will never be the dad I need to be. If I am not encouraged, I will never be the husband my wife needs to lead my family. I love being around people, talking with strangers, and getting to know their stories, but I must have my time alone with God to stay full of love, grace, and hope.

Discouragement is running rampant in our world today. More than ever before, people are depressed, they have no passion for life, and they are running on empty. We need hope! When we lose hope, we lose the ability to dream. How many of you have given up on your dream? How many of you have gotten sidetracked and are bogged down in a spiritual rut? Are you in that place in life where despair has replaced joy? Maybe anxiety has slipped in and replaced your prayer life. When spouses lose hope, they give up on their marriages. When parents lose hope, we give up on our kids; things worsen. When leaders lose hope, they give up on people.

I want to encourage you today, if you are running on fumes and struggling in life, slow down and go to the feet of Jesus. Even though He knows all about you, tell Him how you feel. Ask Him to clean you up and forgive you of all the junk piled up in your life. Then tell Him, "Thank you." Then before you run off from His presence, ask Him to fill you with the Holy Spirit to the point of overflowing. Ask Him to supply you with peace, joy, and hope. The greatest gift you can give your family today is hope. It's not a new house or a new boat. But they need you to be encouraged; they need you to be full of joy. Because the presence of hope creates more satisfied relationships in the family unit., you will be more productive and will be less affected by stress. When you are full of hope, compassion will flow from your life, and you will be more likely to see the blessings of God. Get hope today that only comes from a personal relationship with Jesus. I will ask you that same question again; What are you full of today? Get hope.

~86~
Be Strong And Take Heart

Psalm 31:24 says, "Be strong and take heart, all you who hope in the Lord."

When we have hope, anything is possible. Now that is the truth I am sharing with you today. When parents become hopeful about their kids, they will find new energy for living. When we become confident about our health and start with daily exercises, we get on a positive path to health. So not only should we, as Christians, have hope, but we should also be full and overflowing with hope.

John 3:30 says, "He must become greater; I must become less."

God is calling His Church to be Hope Dealers. Not only are we to receive hope, but we are to give it away. Why do we need hope today? Because hope sets us free from regrets, past hurts, guilt, and bitterness. Hope helps us to bounce back from life situations that have knocked us down. Almost every great Biblical man and woman of God had to bounce back from something. Hope also sets you free to dream. Nobody ever receives a dream from God without having hope. Hope is also the fuel that makes this world a better place. Jesus brought us hope when he overcame sin and death; when he arose from the grave and ascended to the Father's right hand, true hope was born.

Not many people talk about hope today, yet it is something that we all need more of in this unbelievable world today. Hope is not some unreliable sensation or just positive thinking. Hope isn't just wishful thinking or just an unnecessary luxury. We all get discouraged from time to time. Yes, we all get knocked down, overwhelmed, and defeated. But thank God, He has given us hope in Jesus Christ to get back up, overcome, and pull off the victory.

> *First Timothy 6:17 tells us, "Command those who are rich in this present world not to be arrogant nor to put hope in wealth, which is so uncertain, but to put their hope in God, who richly provides us everything for our enjoyment."*

I want to encourage you today to be strong, take heart, and be full of hope. The things of this life will eventually tear up or break down. So make sure to invest in those things that last forever. Begin to enjoy this life and not just get by.

~87~
One Of Those Weeks

It has been a crazy week. I seemed to get a lot done, but so much was happening around me that it was hard to stay focused. We just moved to Titusville, Florida, six months ago, and it has been an awesome experience, and I can't wait to see what God is going to do. But we have been working on the house for six months, cleaning, redoing the kitchen and floors, and revamping the yards. We have more projects on the list but not enough money to complete it all. I keep reminding myself; Rome wasn't built in a day. Little by little.

This week, I had two older friends pass away. Both of these older gentlemen were respected and dearly loved. We all know they are in a better place, praising God in perfect health. But it doesn't make it any easier for family and friends because a piece of them has left this earth. It's hard to watch your friends grieve.

As you know, Covid has raised its ugly head again, and I had good friends and family touched by this round of sickness. Everybody I know has been sick in one way or another. Then you have the everyday stuff that happens on any given day, the car needs new tires, the air conditioner just went out at the house, and the car insurance just came in the mail. Have you ever noticed that they seem to come in threes when bad things begin to happen? All this stuff adds up; it takes a toll on you. Not that you had an awful week, but you get to the end of the week and are emotionally, physically, mentally, and spiritually drained. It's been one of those weeks.

When people ask why bad things happen to good people, we must realize that the worst possible thing happened only once. And Jesus volunteered for it. So, I want to give you Psalm 150 and encourage you to read it when things seem to crumble around you, read it over again when things get hard, and you feel all along. Reread it when you are down and depressed or when you are so tired of not feeling good.

> *Psalm 150:1-6 says, "Praise the Lord. Praise God in his sanctuary; praise him in his mighty heavens. Praise him for his acts of power; praise him for his surpassing greatness. Praise him with the sounding of the trumpet, praise him with the harp and lyre, praise him with tambourine and dancing, praise him with the strings and flute, praise him with clash of cymbals. Let everything that has breath praise the Lord. Praise the Lord."*

Did you catch the message of this scripture? We are to praise him! When you are down and out, praise Him. When you are overwhelmed with sorrow, praise Him. Praise Him when the bills are coming in, and you struggle to pay the house payment. He deserves our praise today, and He is worthy of it all. I challenge you to sing the Lord a new song, kick the tempo, and turn the volume up. You may have had a tough week, but don't forget that Jesus paid the ultimate price to give us life. He deserves our praise.

~88~

Stay Fueled

Running out of gas is frustrating; I have run out several times. Every time it has been when I was cutting grass. To me, nothing is more frustrating than almost being done mowing your yard, you only have a few more strips to cut, and your lawnmower starts to sputter. Then I have to go inside, get my wallet and keys, grab the gas can, and head to the curb store to back up my gas can. The whole time I thought to myself, I could be done now if I had remembered to keep my can full. I hate running out of gas.

Isaiah 40: 30-31 says, "Even young men grow tired and weary, and young men stumble and fall; but those who hope in the Lord will renew their strength. They will soar on wings like eagles; they will run and not grow weary, they will walk and not faint."

Here is my question today: What fuels you? What keeps you going? You can be the most gifted and experienced person in the world, but if you run out of fuel, you will crash and burn. Refueling is so essential for believers in Jesus Christ. In Matthew chapter 14, we find Jesus feeding the five thousand; He took the time to love people, shake hands, and perform a great miracle.

Notice what Jesus did in Matthew 14:22-23, "Immediately Jesus made the disciples get into the boat and go on ahead of him to the other side, while he dismissed them, he went up to a mountainside by himself to pray. When evening came, he was there alone."

Jesus ensured he had plenty of fuel in his spiritual gas can to get the job done. So he went to the soul-filling station of God.

I will change gears and ask you another question: What or who drains you? I had a pool that was constantly losing water. I must put water back in the pool every two or three days. Instead of finding and fixing the leak, I keep filling it with water. I put off taking care of the small tear in my liner, and it cost me greatly. That small tear became significant; then, I had to replace the entire liner of my pool. We must identify what drains us and take the time to fix the issues, not put them off. Be aware of unhealthy people, unkind critics, unbalanced schedules, unnecessary guilt, and exposure to negativity.

I encourage you to invest in your growth, worship, dive into the Word of God, build great relationships, and pay attention to the voices you are listening to. Stay fueled and keep your gas can topped off because you never know when your neighbor's lawn mower will start to sputter. You could save him a trip. So, make a daily trip to the soul-filling station and stay fueled.

~89~
An Attitude Change

Has anyone ever approached you and said, "You need an attitude change?" How many of us have lost that sense of believing God for the impossible? The church will be dead and lifeless until we start believing impossible things are possible with God. Matthew 19:26 Jesus says to his disciples:

> *"With man this is impossible, but with God all things are possible."*

One of the most powerful statements that Jesus spoke in the Book of John is found in John 14:12. I want you to notice that this is written in red, which means that Jesus spoke these very words. Jesus said:

> *"I tell you the truth, anyone who has faith in me will do what I have been doing. He will do even greater things than these because I am going to the Father."*

I have to be honest with you; these words of Jesus blow me out of the water. So, I want to challenge you this morning and encourage you to read back over this verse, then ask the Lord what this means for your life. There are five attitudes that we need to adopt if we are going to live out John 14:12.

- **First, we have to start believing that impossible things are possible.**

  Jesus spoke in Matthew 17:20 and said, "I tell you the truth, if you have faith as small as a mustard seed, you can say to this mountain, 'Move from here to there' and it will move. Nothing will be impossible for you."

- **Secondly, we must believe that God has a better day ahead.**

We can't get stuck in a holding pattern of negativity and routine.

- **Thirdly, we must realize the power of perspective.**

Most of us are waiting for a change of circumstance, but we need a shift in perspective. In Nehemiah's day, Jerusalem was a disaster; for 92 years, the city was in ruins. The people were stuck for ninety-two years without dreams, hope, or a city wall to protect them from enemies. Nehemiah caught a vision of God, then he waited and prayed. When Nehemiah saw a vision of God, he started working on the wall. Fifty-two days later, the wall was built. What changed? One guy showed up with raised expectations, and the city changed forever.

- **Fourthly, we have to replace fear with faith.**

We all know the story of David and Goliath. Everybody in camp expected nothing but defeat, but David expected nothing but victory. The people thought Goliath was too big to defeat, while David thought Goliath was too big to miss.

Don't be so focused on life's problems, but on the God who holds your life in His hand. Don't expect defeat but anticipate God's help. Don't run from difficulty; cover it in prayer and allow God to prepare you to overcome it. Never forget that God is bigger, no matter what you are going through.

- **Finally, stop playing the "what if game."**

Instead of saying "What if," say "Why not?" Give it a try. There will always be those people who want to find a problem. Trust me. I want to challenge you to be the person who finds the solution to the issues. It's time for an attitude change today.

~90~

Walk Like Jesus

First John 2:3-6: "We know that we have come to know him if we obey his commands. The man who says, 'I know him,' but does not do what he commands is a liar, and the truth is not in him. This is how we know we are in him: Whoever claims to live in him must walk as Jesus walked."

Here is the crazy question for today: Are you spending your time and effort each day in a way that would put a smile on God's face? Another way to ask that question is: Are you walking like Jesus? I am so serious; how does your life compare with the life of Christ as you live out your twenty-four-hour day? I hope you can catch what I am trying to put in front of you today. Then, as you chew on that, ask God to help you through the rest of this devotion.

Here is my challenge for you today. I want you to ask God for two things today: First, ask God to give you a hunger for His Word and for the things of God. Growing up as a child, I was skinny as a rail. I ate my food, but mealtime was something I had to do as a child. As I aged, I wanted to put on some size, and I wanted to become stronger. So I had to increase my calories. I had to start eating more and more food. I remember eating a full meal, forcing myself to eat a second portion, and drinking a chocolate shake with two raw eggs. Initially, I had to force myself to eat all that, but in time I desired all that and more. The second thing I want you to pray for is an opportunity to give your faith away.

Ask Him to open the doors of your heart and shutters of your eyes. Ask Him to help you take your eyes off yourself long enough to see the people around you. Get that flow of God moving in your life today. Don't put it off or make excuses. Look for opportunities to encourage, comfort, and teach.

Remember, teaching is not necessarily standing in front of a classroom with a lesson plan. But it is helping other people to walk through life and helping them to discover the goodness of God. Be willing to give away what God has taught you over the years. We can't keep these truths to ourselves; we need that outlet! The greater the intake, the greater the outflow. The more you receive, the more you can give away. He has created us to have this continual flow in our life. This continual flow brings Life to you and those around you. Don't back down from this challenge today; He is trying to push you through a rough spot that has you bogged down spiritually. Hang in there; He is right there by your side.

More Books By Dennis Taylor

1. **Fuel For Today:** A 6-Month Devotional Guide For Spiritual Growth And Encouragement
2. **The Total Package:** The Balanced Life
3. **Fuel For Today Volume 2:** A 3-Month Devotional Guide For Spiritual Growth And Encouragement.
4. **Surrendered:** From Stressed To Blessed; Your Best Life In Jesus' Easy Yoke
5. **He Fills My Cup:** A 90-Day Devotional To Refresh And Restore Your Soul; Drink From The Fountain.
6. **Say It Again:** For The Ones On The Front Row
7. **Temptation In Seven Stages**

About The Author

I started in Student Ministry when I was twenty years old, and it has been my calling for nearly thirty years. My heart was for students to come to know Christ and to grow in their relationship with Him. I love to see God's light bulb fill their eyes and hearts, and I loved sharing the Gospel of Jesus with students whom everybody else said were a lost cause. My passion was to teach them about a relationship with the Lord and give them a real-life example of what it looked like to be walked out in everyday life. My time alone with God has always been my rock, fortress, and high tower. Spending time praying each morning, reading God's Word, and listening to His voice has changed my life forever. I love sharing with young believers who dare to dive deep into the river of God's love. It is so rewarding to invest in the life of other people, watching them go from the shallow end of faith and dive into the deep water of a love relationship with Jesus.

I had the privilege of pastoring two churches, a great blessing to my family and me. First, the Lord led us to plant a church in Leesburg, Georgia. It was a time of growth and a time of great joy. I loved preaching God's Word weekly and encouraging and loving families. We started with twelve people in our home one Sunday morning; a short time later, God opened the door to purchase a building on a couple of acres in Lee County. That church is still going strong and is known as Forrester Community Church. I also had the privilege of pastoring Salem Baptist Church in Worth County, Georgia. Salem is a small country church with a huge heart for God and its community. I was there briefly, but they have a special place in my heart.

Today, I serve as the Pastor of Sports and Recreation at Park Avenue in Titusville, Florida. Peter Lord was the founding pastor of Park Avenue Baptist Church. He was also the author of several well-known books such as Hearing God, Soul Care, 959 Plan, and many more. In addition, he was one of the greatest communicators of God's Word I have ever heard. As the Senior High Student Pastor, I was honored to be discipled by this great man of God in 2004. My role today at Park Avenue is to use sports and recreation to reach out to the community around us. As we develop relationships through sports, God opens the door to share our Jesus with them and their families. My hope, joy, and calling are to lead as many people as possible into a saving relationship with Jesus. Then encourage them to take those next steps to grow and mature in their faith.

In 2022 I wrote two devotional books, Fuel for Today Volumes One and Two. I also penned the book The Total Package, which deals with living a balanced life in Christ. My last two-chapter books were Say It Again and Surrendered, and my previous devotional is He Fills My Cup. I married Laura, my high school sweetheart, and we have been happily married for 36 years. The Lord has blessed us with two grown kids; Carsen serves in the Children's ministry at Passion City Church in Atlanta, Georgia. Mackenzie just got married and is currently working in Augusta, Georgia.

www.ingramcontent.com/pod-product-compliance
Lightning Source LLC
Chambersburg PA
CBHW072003040426
42447CB00009B/1466